W9-CLA-633

SIX INCHES OF
PARTLY CLOUDY

CELEBRATING 50 YEARS ON TV

SIX INCHES OF PARTLY CLOUDY

*Cleveland's Legendary Meteorologist
Takes on Everything—and More*

DICK GODDARD

with Tom Feran

GRAY & COMPANY, PUBLISHERS
CLEVELAND

TO KIM, THE BEST DAUGHTER A DAD COULD HAVE

And to my best friends, Mickey, Butch, Queenie, Boots, Buster, Duke, Mike, Puddles, Wally, Penny, Jack, Li'l Bit, Missy, Lyra, Talan, Dazzle, Tanzen, Tiger Lily, Sienna, Sky, Blueberry, Floozie, Angel, Autumn, Trixie, Tiger, Freddie, Justice, Mercy, Bunnie, Peace, Kieffa, Rhayn, Doppler Dot.Com, Bobbi, Sticky Bun, Templeton, Brownie, Sasha, Luke, and Keaira.

My love for animals—the four-footed and the feathered flock—has no bounds. There is, however, no truth to the rumor that after humanely trapping and releasing mice in my garage, I have them spayed or neutered. But it's not a bad idea.

© 2011 Dick Goddard

All rights reserved. No part of this book may be reproduced or transmitted in any form or by any means, electronic or mechanical, including photocopying, recording, or by any information storage and retrieval system, without written permission of the publisher.

Photos are courtesy of Fox8 TV or from the author's collection except where otherwise noted.

Gray & Company, Publishers
www.grayco.com

Library of Congress Cataloging-in-Publication Data
Goddard, Dick
Six inches of partly cloudy : Cleveland's legendary meteorologist takes on everything—and more / Dick Goddard and Tom Feran.
1. Goddard, Dick 2. Meteorologists—Ohio—Cleveland—Biography. 3. Television weathercasters—Ohio—Cleveland—Biography. 4. WJW-TV (Television station : Cleveland, Ohio)—Biography. 5. Cleveland (Ohio)—Biography. 6. Quotations. I. Feran, Tom. II. Title.
QC858.G63A3 2011
 551.5092—dc22   [B   2011006560

ISBN: 978-1-59851-066-9

Printed in the United States of America
10 9 8 7 6 5 4 3 2 1

CONTENTS

Foreword by Tim Taylor 7

Preface by Tom Feran 10

Introduction 11

Swimming With Sharks 13

Television and Me 23

Words on War 41

What Are You Afraid Of? 47

True Lies 49

The Ohio Country Myth 52

Go Bucks! 58

Snowbelt Diary 61

Lore and Lure of the Woollybear 6 5

Fox 8 Pet Parade 74

Starry, Starry Nights 78

School Daze 83

Weather Wisdom According to Kids 86

Believing Goddard 89

Global Warming 113

When Your Tang Gets Toungled 121

Gossip 129

Pets 134

(Cleveland Press Collection, Cleveland State University Archives)

FOREWORD
by Tim Taylor

Taking nothing away from such Cleveland media icons as "Dorothy," "Barnaby," or "Ghoulardi," "Dick" is simply the most beloved personality in the history of Cleveland broadcasting. Dick Goddard has gone from being Northeast Ohio's favorite uncle to its cherished grandfather. In short, Dick Goddard is the man—a title he sometimes wears uncomfortably and with great humility. Still very much a country boy from Green, Dick combines an innate love of animals and compassion for those less fortunate with a devilish sense of humor reminiscent of Peck's Bad Boy or Eddie Haskell, whose pranks always get everyone else in trouble while leaving him unscathed.

No one would know that better than I do. For three decades I was privileged to have a front-row seat to both the public and private lives of the grand poobah of Cleveland weather. You could say I was either privileged or hilariously victimized by such proximity to the man I still address affectionately as "Goddard"—to which he always replies, "Whatard?"

The king of the Woollybear Festival doesn't just enjoy the chaos that normally accompanies a live television newscast, he revels in it. In fact, the more chaos he can create during the most serious moments of a news broadcast,

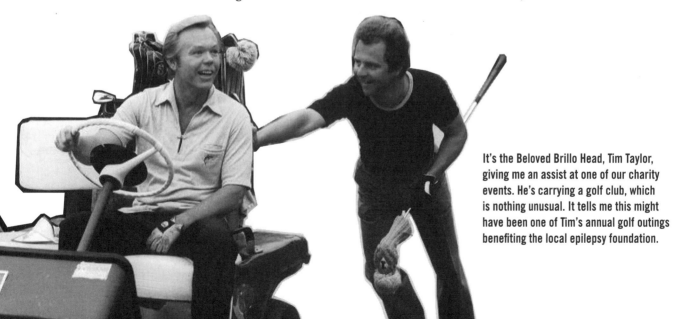

It's the Beloved Brillo Head, Tim Taylor, giving me an assist at one of our charity events. He's carrying a golf club, which is nothing unusual. It tells me this might have been one of Tim's annual golf outings benefiting the local epilepsy foundation.

Were my maker to grant me but one single glance through these sightless eyes of mine, I would without question or recall choose to see first a child, then a dog.

—HELEN KELLER

the more rewarding his day. Many of Dick's most incredible antics both professionally and socially are alone worth the price of this book.

But he also had an uncanny knack of getting himself in trouble on the air, often describing his many on-camera predicaments as talking himself into a verbal cul de sac. Sometimes it went far beyond a simple stumble. Only weeks before I retired at the end of 2005, Dick unwittingly provided me with a going-away gift that just keeps on giving because it now tops my very long list of Goddard stories.

As fall turned to winter, Dick lamented to his faithful viewers that he always feared the dreaded spoonerism at the approach of each new winter, when he'd be faced with saying "cold air mass" several hundred times for the next few months. Only this time, what he was thinking overrode his tongue, and he actually uttered what he was always afraid of saying, which was "cold mare's ass." For a moment there was nothing but shocked silence, followed by Goddard confirming what we all thought we had heard. "Oh my God . . . I said it!" Howls of laughter filled the studio and much of the Fox 8 building. But as you're about to read, this was only the latest reason that Dick's forecasts have always been must-watch television.

In the late 1960s I put away my paintbrushes and started using magnets on my WJW weather maps.

Dick's love and dedication to animals has been well documented. But his innate goodness and generosity also extends to people. Over the years it sometimes has made him a target, but again, not without humor. Such as the time Dick, Robin, and I were about to enter our favorite take-out eatery and a man approached with his young son, instinctively looking to Dick for the money they needed to buy dinner. Dick generously offered to take them inside with us and buy them dinner. The man never blinked when he responded that he'd rather have the money because they wanted to go Chinese.

Dick's propensity for investing in questionable schemes and businesses is also legendary. Dragging his close friends along with him has also cost me a few bucks over the years, causing some colleagues to suggest that our investing mission statement might easily be *buy high, sell low*.

Dick's love and dedication to animals has been well documented

To be fair, Goddard's friendship did change my personal fortunes when he hooked me up with his high-powered agent, the late Ed Keating. The big Irishman had already made his bones in the rough-and-tumble world of negotiating with the billionaire owners of football and baseball teams. Keating, in fact, successfully pulled off the first tandem contract in NFL history, involving running backs Larry Csonka and Jim Kiick of the Miami Dolphins. And on the wall behind Keating's desk hung a blown-up multimillion dollar check he negotiated for Hall of Fame reliever Dennis Eckersley.

I tell you this because, for all of Keating's celebrated negotiating savvy, he could never quite figure out how to control Dick's appetite for, shall we say, interesting investments. Keating would call in a state of exasperation and panic, asking how we ever got involved in "another hare-brained scheme" that always reminded him of Ralph Kramden and Ed Norton.

As you're about to learn, Dick Goddard is appropriately as unpredictable and uncontrollable as Cleveland's weather. And that's why contributing to a book about his fascinating life was irresistible. I think you'll agree that Dick Goddard was, is, and always will be Cleveland's own, one-of-a-kind, exalted Cleveland weather guru—and, oh, so much more. Enjoy the stories!

PREFACE
by Tom Feran

I tracked Hurricane Gladys on the weather board at KYW in September 1964. I'm holding a piece of chalk, which is what I used to mark the map. It took hours to do it, and after four years I was on the verge of white lung disease. I would chalk four hours a day.

Television's history is crowded with "firsts," "mosts," and "longests." Most of those records have asterisks attached to them, indicating that they apply to one particular station, network, city, or state. And then there is Dick Goddard, who has had the longest career as a TV weather forecaster in history. Not just at TV8, or in Cleveland, or in Ohio, but the longest career anywhere. Period. No asterisk. His true peers are a handful of legendary meteorologists who had remarkable careers in a field as fickle as the weather itself.

Harold Taft was the first TV meteorologist west of the Mississippi (and one of only three in the country), when he started forecasting for Dallas–Fort Worth in 1949 on WBAP (later KXAS). Dubbed "World's Greatest Weatherman" on the all-night "Road Gang" radio show for truckers, he was the longest-serving TV meteorologist in the world when he retired after forty-one years and ten months in August 1991.

Woody Assaf was an original staffer at WLBT in Jackson, Mississippi, when it signed on the air in December 1953. When he ended his career in August 2001 after forty-eight years, he was recognized as the longest-serving weatherman at one station in the history of television.

And there is Canada's Dave Devall. When the former Royal Canadian Air Force meteorologist retired from CFTO-TV in Toronto on April 3, 2009, Guinness World Records and the World Records Academy announced that he held the newly created record for "longest career as a weather forecaster": forty-eight years, two months, and twenty-seven days.

Dick Goddard tops that. He made his TV forecasting debut on May 1, 1961, which made May 1, 2011, his fiftieth anniversary on television. Except for nine months when he went to Philadelphia with KYW-TV, and then was under contract with TV8 but waiting out a "no-compete" agreement, he spent all fifty years on the air in Cleveland, watching the winds aloft and the woollybears.

Entering his fifty-first year in television, he is the world's longest-serving TV forecaster and the undisputed dean of Cleveland television. It is highly unlikely that anyone will ever do it longer, or even come close.

It is certain that no one will do it better.

INTRODUCTION
by Dick Goddard

It was the early 1940s, and down on our little farm south of Akron (now the city of Green) I was lying on my bed with my tail-wagging friends, Boots and Buster. We had just listened to Jack Graney broadcasting the Cleveland Indians game. On clear nights my little Zenith radio could ever so faintly pick up the legendary Red Barber, voice of the Brooklyn Dodgers.

While trying to dial up the Dodgers I came across a late-night radio preacher who was in spiritual high dudgeon and warning everyone about the new evil that was spreading across the land: TELEVISION! From his electronic bully pulpit the minister proclaimed that television was the work of the devil, since God never intended for pictures to fly through the air. The preacher warned that anyone who was watching or connected with Satan's tool would be destined to spend eternity in a fiery furnace.

"LOOKS LIKE A NICE DAY."

Since, like everyone else, I was fascinated by those fuzzy, flickering images on six-inch black-and-white television screens, I was consoled by the thought that I would be wearing asbestos underwear with my TV friends Kukla, Fran, and Ollie.

For fifty years I have been tumbling and flying through the atmosphere and into living rooms and bedrooms throughout Northeast Ohio. And it has been a dizzying—and delightful—journey. What follows are some of the highlights from my wicked and sinful career on the boob tube. With my TV tales—and cartoons—I hope to make you smile.

I'm sure that I'll raise a few hackles with some of my opinions, as well. I subscribe to the adage that "If you don't want to be criticized, say nothing, do nothing, be nothing."

Here goes nothing.

When you are born you cry and the world laughs. Live your life so that when you die, you laugh and the world cries.

Dad took me to Michigan every summer to fish, and I was pulling them in at age four. A corncob pipe completed my fishing gear. I actually did smoke a pipe for awhile, but gave it up in 1973.

Swimming with Sharks

It was the old Notre Dame football coach Frank Leahy who said, "I'd rather be lucky than good." I have been one lucky fellow. I grew up in Green, a farm community just north of Massillon. It's a city now, but it was Greensburg at the time. Before that, back in the early 1900s, it was Inland. If you look at a map, you'll see Greensburg, Pennsylvania; Greensburg, Ohio; and Greensburg, Indiana, all at the same latitude. The pioneers would name a community and say, "This is a good name, but too many people are coming in. We're gonna get out of here. We're gonna move west." So they did, and they named the new place Greensburg.

We lived on a five-acre farm, growing vegetables. It would be called a truck farm. We had a stand out front, and I'd be required to go out and sell stuff. I hated it. If anybody bought a dozen ears of corn, they would get eighteen because I wanted to get rid of the stuff as soon as I could.

Right across the street from us was a huge chicken ranch. They had thousands of chickens, and would eventually decapitate and de-feather them. For two summers I had the job, for about fifty cents an hour, of cleaning out the buildings where all the you-know-what from the chickens was, in huge pyramids. In the hot sun those piles took on a life of their own. They began to glisten and move. After two years of doing that I decided I didn't want to get into solid waste management. I haven't had chicken since, or anything with feathers.

I'm pretty much a vegetarian—I don't even eat animal crackers. But I'm not vegan, and I love cheese. And I don't eat coleslaw because nothing to this day compares to my mother's coleslaw. My mom was a great cook.

Happy Trails Farm has a wide variety of animals, including the aptly named Wild Bill.

I haven't had chicken since, or anything with feathers.

Sportcaster Jim Graner and news anchor Pat Murray were two of my partners on Channel 3's *Eyewitness News*. Both were funny guys. They would laugh so much at each other that one had to leave the set when the other was doing the news so they wouldn't break up on camera.

With eyes upraised his master's look to scan, the joy, the solace and the aid of man; the rich man's guardian and the poor man's friend, the only creature faithful to the end.

—ANONYMOUS

My dad was mechanic, and very good at his job. He worked for Railway Express Agency, and what a tight outfit that was. My mom said he never took a promotion into management because he couldn't fire anybody; that's what a kind soul he was. He was an exemplar of honesty. They were wonderful people. Neither made it past the fourth grade, but they were the most honest, kind, and hard-working people you could imagine. They had common sense and reason, which trumps all the degrees and certificates of achievement that hang on walls.

Sportsman

I was an only child, so my imagination came into play. I liked to go to school because I had friends here. Back on our little farm, I was making up games. I'd throw a ball up against the house, making up baseball games. (I never broke a window, but I did break some siding.) I'd broadcast the games to myself, too, announcing them the way I heard on the radio, listening to Jack Graney do the Indians games with his sidekick, Pinky Hunter.

They used some imagination, too, because they didn't travel with the team. For away games, they would use a telegraph wire. There would be a long pause, and you'd hear information coming in on ticker tape. During away games in World War II, if it began to rain, they couldn't say what the problem was. They'd say, well, the game now has been suspended, apparently because they figured the Germans or the Japanese were listening in, and if they knew it was raining it would be a problem. In 1944, they couldn't broadcast games because they didn't have a sponsor on the radio. Finally Bug-a-boo came to our rescue, the bug spray. I'd listen to Detroit games, where Harry Heilmann was the announcer, and Pittsburgh. Television wasn't even a rumor when I was in high school, but by the time I was a senior, television had come in.

I loved football. Well, growing up near Massillon, of course I did. I think any newborn male still gets a football in the hospitals there. We scrimmaged Massillon once in football, and that was a big mistake. We were a Class B school. The coach scheduled this thing with Massillon, and as we were in the locker room I questioned it. The coach said, "Now remember, those people put their pants on the same way we do." I said, "Yeah, but their waist size is, like, 42." "You're a smartass, Goddard."

A promotional ad boasting Channel 3's expanded *Eyewitness News*. It was a long day for me then—I was on the news at noon, 7 p.m., and 11 p.m.

DICK'S MEMORIES

Leg Man

Bill Jorgensen, the first evening news anchor I worked with at KYW, debuted the first live newsroom cut-in in 1961. It was a shaky start, since unknown to Bill, in the background behind him, the assignment editor and a cameraman were having a fist fight.

Bill was also one of the first TV news anchors to stand while reporting. He had enjoyed communing with nature over the weekend when nature called. With no paper at hand, he grabbed a clump of grass, which unfortunately contained a goodly amount of poison ivy. He stood for several weeks.

Bill often came to work in summer wearing the standard suit and tie—and shorts. That worked well until the night the flimsy anchor desk collapsed on the air, revealing his unique anchorman attire. That was the last time for shorts.

A display of gauges was a high-tech touch on KYW's weather set in 1962.

I was a tailback and a single-wing, and I played baseball, too—third base. In basketball we were Class B champions my senior year. We had good teams.

I survived a tryout with the Brooklyn Dodgers, right after my senior year. There were two hundred kids in Akron at Firestone Park. They asked me and twelve other kids to come back the next day, but none of my buddies were asked so I didn't go. I'm sure Spider Jorgensen, who played third base for the Dodgers, felt very secure I wasn't playing. But I got a hit off Akron's number-one pitcher, one of the best players ever in Akron, Dick Hamlin. That's my claim to baseball fame.

Being a football nut, I saw the first Browns game ever, in August 1946, in Akron. I bought my buddy a ticket and we both went. The Rubber Bowl was filled. For about twenty-five years the Browns opened at the Rubber Bowl. They used to play six exhibition games. Now they're down to four. They'll probably cut it down to three, which makes more sense.

After graduation from high school in 1949, the Korean "conflict" (it seemed like a real war) dictated service to my country. I enlisted in the United States Air Force. My goal since childhood, however, was to be a cartoonist for Walt Disney. (I still have the Donald Duck I drew when I was five years old.)

Following basic training at Sampson Air Force Base, I was given the standard aptitude test that would determine the job I would have for the next four years. Unfortunately, I found there were no openings for cartoonists in the military. Since I qualified as a "sharpshooter," the air force said I was a candidate for gunnery school. No thanks. The lieutenant who administered

Going to church no more makes you a Christian than standing in a garage makes you a car.

—GARRISON KEILLOR

my qualifications then told me that I was suited for meteorology school. I accepted, even though my only experience and interest with weather was that I had been out in it.

While a number of my fellow weather school graduates were immediately sent to Korea, the air force—in their wisdom—sent me to Greenland. Don't laugh. In the twelve months I was there, not one North Korean made it into Greenland. They knew better.

After Greenland, I was assigned to the 6th Mobile Weather Squadron at Tinker AFB in Oklahoma. This led to the greatest adventure in my military career. I was one of six meteorologists that supported the Atomic Energy Commission on the first full-yield hydrogen bomb test at Enewetak (then Eniwetok) in the Pacific islands (see "A Glimpse of Hell"). I met Edward Teller, "father of the H-bomb," in the weather office.

In 1971, WJW's anchor team was, from left, sportscaster Dave Martin, news anchors Marty Ross and Murray Stewart, and me. Martin also called Indians games on TV8 from 1969 to 1971 with Harry Jones.

After being discharged, I entered Kent State University in pursuit of a Bachelor of Fine Arts degree. It took five years of working nights at the U.S. Weather Bureau at the Akron-Canton airport, but I finally made it. It was the weather broadcasts on local radio stations that prompted KYW television in Cleveland to call and offer me a chance to audition. I initially said "no thanks," since I had taken no courses in the KSU communications department and only one speech course. I was eminently unqualified for television. Besides, we were all air force or navy vets at the Weather Bureau, and we thought we were a big deal because we were on the radio down there. We had about three stations in Canton and Akron.

When KYW called again, several weeks later—and at the urging of my weather friends—I told them I would give the tube a try. (Ironically, I received a favorable response from Walt Disney productions in California the same week.) I became the first meteorologist on Cleveland television. A storm really opened the door for me. It was Hurricane Donna in 1960.

I had been doing my radio reports on Hurricane Donna, a huge, slow-moving storm that hit nearly every state on the East Coast. KYW called the next week. The general manager, George Mathieson, had been driving to Akron for a speech when he heard this young guy on the radio, who seemed to know what he was talking about. They were looking for a meteorologist because Don Kent had been so successful on their Westinghouse sister station in Bos-

DICK'S PALS

A Soft Touch

TIM TAYLOR: People see Dick and they bring him hard-luck stories. He's a soft touch for people in trouble, almost as much as animals. We were going out to dinner at Wendy's between shows one evening, and it was heartbreaking. There was a guy with his kid outside. The guy comes up to Dick and says, "Can you spare some money for my son and I? We're really hungry." Dick goes, "Well, I'll tell you what—I'll take you. Come with us into Wendy's, and we'll buy you dinner." The guy said, "I'd rather have the cash. We want to go Chinese."

Tim Taylor worked beside Dick Goddard as TV8's chief anchor from 1977 to 2005. Much honored for his broadcast journalism in a career spanning five decades, Tim also took a justified and gleeful measure of pride in being, at one time, Cleveland's only main male anchor with his own hair.

If animals could speak, the dog would be a blunt, outspoken fellow, but the cat would have the rare talent of never saying a word too much.

—PHILIP HAMERTON

Drive On

ROBIN SWOBODA: Dick can be tranquilly oblivious. We were driving back from Muscular Dystrophy camp once, and the Highway Patrol had a speed trap on the side of the road with a radar gun. They started waving us over. Dick drives right on by. I said, "Dick, I think we were supposed to pull over." "Well, how do you know, Robby?" I said, "Well, they were waving us over and other people were pulling over." He said, "Hmm," and kept driving. He claims he called later and turned himself in.

Robin Swoboda has been Dick Goddard's friend and sometime comic foil ever since she joined WJW-TV8 as Tim Taylor's co-anchor in 1986.

ton, WBZ. The Westinghouse stations were looking for guys who had some exposure to isobars. That was the entrée I had.

My audition at KYW went on for weeks in 1960. When I was done, others would follow me into the studio. I'm sure I was terrible, but the others were evidently worse. I was ready to call it quits when the TV station called to say they would offer me a thirteen-week contract. That's how sure they were that I'd be staying around. My dad urged me to turn down the offer since there was a good chance that I'd be swimming with sharks. I jumped in anyway.

KYW actually took me on a test run in December of 1960 when they put me on Linn Sheldon's "Barnaby" show. I brought my pet raccoon, Freddie, with me from the farm. He was a big hit. Barnaby and Dorothy Fuldheim, Big Red, were Cleveland's most popular personalities at the time. Barnaby had already been on KYW for years, and he confided to me the secret to being a success on television: "Honesty, sincerity, integrity, and the ability to fake all three." Linn was a marvelous entertainer and raconteur.

The first time you are on television is an experience you can't imagine. I've witnessed the H-bomb, I was in a tornado in Akron, I've flown into a hurricane with the U.S. Navy hurricane hunters, and I've flown upside-down with the Air Force Thunderbirds. No big deal. On TV for the first time your whole life passes before your eyes. My initiation came on May 1, 1961, with veteran broadcasters Bud Dancy and Jim Graner. I remember Jim introduced me by saying, "Dick Goddard, the first meteorologist on Cleveland television, will be here with his first rumor in two minutes." When I began, my voice was up several octaves. Some said that small animals began to gather outside the station.

I compounded my shaky television debut with a spoonerism when I referred to the weather legend of croaking frogs as "froaking crogs." As I slumped at my little drafting table in the KYW newsroom, I expected our program director to offer the opinion that "thirteen weeks is a long time." In retrospect, I figured that viewers had to call the station and demand that I stay on the air because I was so entertainingly bad.

I quickly became aware of the animosity that existed between newspaper

In 1963 I flew into Hurricane Flora, one of the deadliest hurricanes in history, with the U.S. Navy Hurricane Hunters, on the first nighttime low-level penetration of a hurricane. Hurricane reconnaissance planes fly through the less violent portion of the storm, usually the southwest quadrant. Going in at less than a thousand feet, we were surrounded by continuous lightning.

Man is the only animal that feels insulted when he is called an animal.

There is one thing we do know. That man is here for the sake of other men—above all for those upon whose smile and well-being our own happiness depends, and also for the countless unknown souls whose fate we are connected with by a bond of sympathy.

—ALBERT EINSTEIN

journalists and those on television. The print reporters and journalists had it all to themselves before the hair-sprayed electronic rivals arrived. While a number of local columnists were kind to me, some were vicious. The radio-TV editor of the *Akron Beacon Journal* relished publishing letters to the editor that ridiculed me. "Don't worry," the TV expert wrote. "He won't be around long." I was embarrassed for my parents and family.

Since I had no previous TV experience, I thought that KYW would send me to some sort of television "charm school." (They have such places, and a friend of mine at a competing Cleveland television station was sent there to "learn to blink," since his eye contact was unrelenting.) In reality, KYW hung me out to dry. It was sink or swim, and thanks to the generosity of viewers, I've been dog paddling ever since.

I've had the good fortune to work with some wonderful news directors, but my first was not one of them. He was very likely the role model for Ed Asner's acerbic character on the classic *Mary Tyler Moore Show*. The guy could have been the front man for a famine. He felt that both weather and sports had no business being on a television news program.

DICK'S MEMORIES

Piddling Prognostication

It was a weekend in late January 1978. Along with Doug Adair and other TV folks, I was at the sled dog race in Geauga County. As we were waiting for the start of the race, a husky came over to Doug and lifted his leg. When the laughter subsided, I kiddingly said, "He must have seen your show." I also related the Eskimo legend that such behavior foretells a coming storm (more laughter). Five days later, the deepest storm in Ohio weather history hit the state. The blizzard of '78 created winds of over 100 miles an hour.

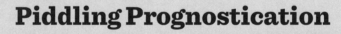

"OONAK IS STILL THE BEST LEAD DOG IN THE BUSINESS".

I had, evidently, collected enough viewers to allow an extension of my initial contract. It was eleven months after being hired that the news director confronted me in the teletype room. He said, "Goddard, they want you over at the Hollenden House tomorrow. They're going to give you an award for whatever you're doing." I said, "I don't believe it!" He said, "Neither do I."

I wasn't on the air long before the program director at KYW took me aside and told me to point out any bad forecasts from the local National Weather Service. I told him that I couldn't do that. The shark swam away.

Everyone in the television news business has stories to tell about the personalities they have met. Following are the memories I treasure.

This is my favorite photo. Those were the days. Cleveland made me, Robin, Tim, and Casey its own. And we were.

During the 1995 World Series, this notorious gang of four were warned by security that they would be thrown out of the Atlanta Braves press box if they kept cheering for the Indians.

they
put it
all
together . . .

The News and Weather,
with meaningful pictures,
and color, and you in
view. It's the next best
thing to being there
yourself, when news
happens. City Camera
News, at Noon,
6 and
11 pm ei8ht WJW-TV

I'm not really old enough to have been photographed with
Abe Lincoln by Matthew Brady. That's Gerald Bestrom of
Michigan, who became a full-time Lincoln impersonator in
1991. The resemblance is striking, though Gerald is an inch
shorter than the sixteenth president's 6 feet, 4 inches. He's
at the Woollybear Festival every year, and he plays "The
Battle Hymn of the Republic" on a saw.

Television and Me

"The problem with television is that people must sit and keep their eyes glued to a screen: the average American family hasn't time for it. Therefore the showmen are convinced that for this reason, if no other, television will never be a serious competitor of radio broadcasting."

—The New York Times, 1939

The popularity of those unrealistic television "reality" programs is a phenomenon that many feel is proof that God never meant for pictures to fly through the air. Today in the United States there are 115 million homes with television, and cable or satellite service is in 88 percent of those homes. Only one in fifty people claims to never watch television.

But whom should we honor—or blame—for the electronic invention that glues millions of Americans to flickering images in a box for an average of four and one-half hours every day of the year?

Did Thomas Edison invent television? No.

How about Albert Einstein? No.

Guglielmo Marconi? No.

In spite of claims by the Radio Corporation of America (RCA) and its former egomaniacal president, David Sarnoff—who founded the National Broadcasting Network—the first television image was created by Philo T. Farnsworth, a humble Dagwood Bumstead–type farm boy, who never received proper recognition for his genius and intellect.

Philo (Phil to friends and family) Farnsworth was born in a log cabin to a dirt-poor family at Beaver, Utah, on August 19, 1906. Seldom smiling, with a slight build and bright blue eyes, Phil had a sandy-brown shock of hair that topped a larger-than-ordinary head and a prominent forehead.

If we knew what we were doing, it wouldn't be called research.

—ALBERT EINSTEIN

I made my television debut on TV3's *Eyewitness News at Noon* on May 1, 1961, with anchor Bud Dancy and sportscaster Jim Graner.

The three-day weekend was created because it's impossible to cram all the bad weather into two days.

—CONVENTIONAL WISDOM

There was no electricity in his home, and Phil rode to school on horseback in the hardscrabble days of his youth. When he was eleven his family loaded their meager possessions into three covered wagons and headed northward into the Snake River Valley at Rigby, Idaho. They moved into the home of Phil's uncle, Albert Farnsworth, on a 240-acre farm with electricity supplied by a Delco generator.

The young man developed an intense interest in science early in life, devouring every radio and electronics magazine he could find. By age fourteen, having memorized Einstein's photoelectric theories, he decided that he would be the one to invent what would become known as television.

It was in early spring 1921 that the epiphany of how television could work came like a lightning bolt out of the blue. Phil had been plowing a potato field on a horse-drawn harrow. As he gazed at the freshly plowed rows of soil, he imagined that electrons (negatively charged elementary particles) could be lined up in the same way in order to scan a picture.

Phil jumped from his seat on the harrow and shouted to his startled father, "Papa, Papa, I've got it!"

Lewis Farnsworth realized that his son had an unusual imagination when, at the age of twelve, Phil announced he could repair the failed electric generator that was so important to the farm operation. Phil understood that by passing a strong magnet along a wire, thereby putting electrons into motion, he could produce electricity. He knew that magnetism and electricity were companions, and that streams of electrons could be manipulated by magnets.

As several of his cousins gathered to laugh at and mock their "Einstein" relative, Phil dismantled and cleaned the generator, made a few adjustments, and pressed the "on" button.

"The damned thing works!" exclaimed his father.

His son's esoteric and deep thinking amazed the elder Farnsworth so much that he made Phil promise to keep his arcane abilities secret. "People think you are a bit odd," said his father, "and this will remove all doubt."

Radio was exploding across the country in the 1920s, and building your own radio crystal set was a very popular subject in science and electronics magazines. Phil knew that the next giant step would be putting moving pictures with the sound. Phil ordered his first crystal set from a Sears Roebuck catalog (the Sears catalog was a young man's treasure, since it gave him his first exposure to such forbidden things as ladies' undergarments). By selling his baby lambs, Phil had also earned enough money to order a violin from the catalog. He became so proficient with the fiddle that his father imagined him as a concert violinist. Phil collected five bucks every Friday night for playing in the band at the high school gymnasium. "Down by the Old Mill Stream" was a favorite tune.

In 1926, at age twenty, Phil Farnsworth continued his dream of inventing television, applying for two basic patents: one for a television camera and the other for the reception of television signals. He called his device an "image dissector." Phil was not alone in his quest, however. Hundreds of scientists working in laboratories around the United States all pursued the holy grail of broadcasting.

Channel 3 news director Phil Lewis was a hard-news guy who had little use for weather and segments. "Goddard," he said to me one day, "they want you over at the Hollenden House tomorrow—they're going to give you an award for whatever you're doing." I said, "I don't believe it!" He said, "Neither do I." This was the award, from the days before local Emmys.

If you pick up a starving dog and make him prosperous, he will not bite you. This is the principal difference between a dog and a man.

—MARK TWAIN

We were a long way from computer-generated graphics at TV8 in the 1960s. I'm wearing a smock, holding a brush, and using fast-drying Tempera paint, a step up from watercolor, to mark the map for my forecast.

Enter a Goliath named David, a five-foot-eight-inch Napoleon with steel-blue eyes.

David Sarnoff had also come from poor and humble beginnings in his native city of Minsk in Russia. His family fled to the United States in the cargo section of a steamship, landing in the slums of New York City on the Lower East Side. His parents had wanted him to become a rabbi, but Sarnoff's fortunes turned when he was able to get a job as a telegraph key operator at the Wall Street offices of the American Marconi Company. By chance he was able to meet Guglielmo Marconi, inventor of the precursor of radio, the wireless telegraph.

Sarnoff curried favor with Marconi and soon became his office gofer. Marconi was a big hit with the ladies, and Sarnoff spent much of his time delivering chocolates and flowers to Marconi's female favorites.

It was on the fateful night of April 14, 1912, while continuing to work as a telegraph operator at American Marconi, that Sarnoff claimed he heard over his earphones the first distress signal from the sinking and doomed luxury liner *Titanic*. An RCA biography later boasted that Sarnoff stayed at his telegraph position for seventy-two straight hours. (Critics have argued that both claims were apocryphal, knowing that Sarnoff was a relentless self-promoter.)

Amid the madcap race for radio broadcast rights, the Radio Corporation of America was founded in 1919. David Sarnoff continued to climb the corporate ladder, becoming RCA's patent policeman. He made sure that it would be against the law for anyone without a license from RCA to build a radio or sell one without paying royalties to his company.

One day in 1928, in the New York RCA headquarters, the thirty-seven-year-old Sarnoff read an article in the *San Francisco Chronicle* about a young independent scientist named Philo Farnsworth who had set up a laboratory in a drafty loft on Green Street at the base of San Francisco's Telegraph Hill.

Never mistake knowledge for wisdom. One helps you make a living, the other helps you make a life.

—SANDRA CAREY

Sarnoff coveted the patent on television and was determined to bully his way toward that goal. He decided to go to San Francisco and meet his rival. Accompanying Sarnoff was Vladimir Zwyorkin, a Russian expatriate engineer who was hired by Sarnoff to develop a television system for RCA. Zwyorkin was well aware of Farnsworth and his work, and he had been developing his own system that he called an "image orthicon," based largely on Farnsworth's principles.

Sarnoff believed that Farnsworth was basically a simple boy genius who—like others under Sarnoff's command—could easily be controlled and bought out cheaply. It was truly David versus Goliath in the battle over a box with lights and wires that eventually would be found in more U.S. homes than indoor plumbing.

Sarnoff swaggered into Farnsworth's San Francisco laboratory with Zwyorkin in tow, swinging his ever-present oak walking stick. Zwyorkin complimented Farnsworth on his accomplishments, and Sarnoff immediately offered Farnsworth $100,000 for his system. Farnsworth turned him down.

From that point it became a battle between Farnsworth's image dissector and Zwyorkin's image orthicon. The war began, and litigation over which side would win the patent raged on for six years. It was the modest resources of Farnsworth and his few investors against the massive fortune of RCA.

The battle took its toll on Farnsworth. Facing bankruptcy, Phil became depressed, his health began to fail, and his relationship with his devoted wife Pam (Elma) deteriorated. Farnsworth began to drink heavily. Finally, in 1936, the courts ruled that Philo was indeed the inventor of television, and he was issued a patent. RCA was ordered to pay him, which infuriated Sarnoff. "We don't pay royalties!" he fumed. "We collect them."

While Farnsworth continued his work in anonymity, and financial rewards were slow in coming, Sarnoff became a national figure, offering the services of RCA during the critical war years of the early 1940s. Sarnoff had been a member of the U.S. Army Reserves in the 1920s, and though he had no real military expe-

In the early 1960s, Channel 3 was KYW-TV, and my forecast was part of *Eyewitness News.*

"I'LL HANDLE THE ANALYSIS, FARNSWORTH!"

The dog guards the sleep of his pauper master as if he were a prince. When all other friends desert, he remains. When riches take wings and reputation falls to pieces, he is as constant in his love as the sun in its journey across the heavens.

—GEORGE GRAHAM VEST

rience, his inside connections resulted in his being given the rank of lieutenant colonel.

Sarnoff had renounced his Russian heritage and declared himself a true patriot of his country. Following the Japanese attack on Pearl Harbor on December 7, 1941, he telegraphed President Franklin Roosevelt from RCA headquarters and pledged that "all our facilities are ready and at your instant service. We await your commands." RCA became an important military contractor during the war, providing radar tubes, sonar systems, and radio transmitters, as well as research and development.

In 1944, with the D-day invasion at hand, Sarnoff was given active-duty status, and he reported directly to General Eisenhower in London. The Allied Forces Network provided communications that were instrumental in coordinating the greatest military operation in history.

For his services, President Roosevelt gave Sarnoff the rank of honorary brigadier general in the U.S. Army. Returning to his headquarters in New York, Sarnoff promptly informed RCA that he was no longer to be addressed as simply Mr. Sarnoff. He was to be called General Sarnoff, or General.

To validate David Sarnoff's colossal ego, in 1950 he asked the Radio and Television Manufacturers Association to bestow upon him the title of "Father of Television." Sarnoff received his self-proclaimed honor, and all RCA employees were informed that the designation was official. Only he was to be so recognized.

Farnsworth, who sought no glory, won his first patent-licensing victory over RCA in 1939, the same year that he was named—along with New York Yankees first baseman Lou Gehrig—as one of the "Outstanding Young Men" in the nation. This would be one of the few national honors he would receive. The last national recognition for Philo Farnsworth, while he was living, came in 1957 on the popular television show *What's My Line?* Panelists on the show were blindfolded as they asked questions of the mystery guest that the studio audience and television viewers could see. When panelist Jayne Meadows inquired, "Does what you do sometimes cause pain?" Farnsworth replied, "Sometimes it does. Yes."

None of the panelists was able to identify Farnsworth as the inventor of

DICK'S PALS

"Am I Saying Goodbye?"

JOE BENNY: In November 2005, a weekend promotional teaser on Fox 8 promised a big announcement on Monday's 6 p.m. news: "Someone will say goodbye."

Tim Taylor laughed as he watched it, and said he was expecting a worried phone call from Dick Goddard.

"He'll think it's him," Taylor said gleefully, before announcing his own retirement from television after twenty-seven years as WJW's prime anchor and forty years in Cleveland broadcasting. "I can hear him: 'Tim, am I saying goodbye?'

"Dick is my dearest friend there, and I can't tell him it's me. He can't keep a secret. I'm going to call him at home and tell him—and I'll tell him why I didn't tell him. And he's going to say, 'It's a good thing you didn't tell me.'"

Joe Benny was executive producer of news at WJW-TV8 for more than twenty years. He currently is district director for U.S. Representative Dennis Kucinich.

It looks like some sort of strange cult, and maybe it is—a whole family of woollybears paying a visit to the weather center at TV8.

Welcome!

ROBIN SWOBODA: I came to TV8 in January 1986 but didn't go on the air until March. I had two months to get acclimated and settle in before Denise D'Ascenzo left. She was late coming in one day, and I saw a cake and people waiting around. Dick waved me into the room. He said, "We're having a 'Welcome to TV8' party for you! Come on in! We're gonna welcome Robin!" He got me a chair, and just then Denise walked in the door.

Dick pulls the chair away and says to me, "Get out!" The party was supposed to be for Denise!

*A cat looks down on a man, a dog looks up to a man, but
a pig will look man right in the eye and see his equal.*

—WINSTON CHURCHILL

"WE NEVER HAD THIS KIND'A WEATHER TILL THEY STARTED SENDING THOSE ROCKS UP!"

television. As a reward for his appearance, Philo Farnsworth was given a carton of Winston cigarettes and eighty dollars. (Curiously, both Farnsworth and Zwyorkin lamented the poor quality of programming during the early years of television. Zwyorkin said the most important part of a television set was the switch that allowed you to turn it off. Farnsworth chided his son for watching too much TV. At one time, none of the eight television sets in the Farnsworth home was working.)

My partners on TV8's *City Camera* in 1973 were Marty Ross and Murray Stewart.

In 1989 elementary school students in Utah became aware of the importance of Philo Farnsworth. It was through their efforts that a statue in his honor is on display in our nation's capital. At the National Statuary Hall in Washington each state is represented by two figures. For the state of Utah there is Brigham Young alongside Philo Taylor Farnsworth. Farnsworth is holding and gazing at an image dissector tube. At the base of his statue there is an inscription: Father of Television.

While denied the wealth that such a monumental invention should have provided, Elma (Pam) Farnsworth, Phil's wife, was able to live out her ninety-two years in financial security following her husband's death at age sixty-four on March 11, 1971. David Sarnoff, who became a multimillionaire while president of RCA, died in his sleep at age eighty on December 12, 1971.

Thank you, Phil Farnsworth, for allowing me to have a great career.

I've been lucky in my career. People have been so good to me, while I've been able to irritate television viewers in twenty-three counties every night. A weather forecast is nothing more than an estimate of probability, and it will never be more than that. And the further ahead you go, the less accurate a forecast is going to be. In Northeast Ohio especially, the best weather forecast you can give is never going to be 100 percent accurate. If it's 80 percent accurate for our viewing area, the other 20 percent are really upset.

Visitors to this country are usually amazed at the time and attention given to weather on television. There are two reasons for this fixation: (1) Ever since God allowed pictures to fly through the air, television executives have found that weather programs are an easy sell; (2) This country has a greater variety of weather than any other, and it is frequently violent.

The popularity of TV weather shouldn't be underestimated. I'm a certified sports nut, and my fellow jock enthusiasts are always surprised when I tell them that surveys continually indicate that the television weather audience is regularly four times as large as the sports audience.

Getting the weather message out to the public hasn't always been easy. Today radio and television broadcasts allow massive and immediate distribution of highly perishable weather forecasts and warnings. There was a time, not so long ago, when weather information was just as much a rumor as the forecast itself. While the government weather service was signed into existence by President Ulysses S. Grant in 1870, the first official forecast was not made until February 19, 1871, by Professor Cleveland Abbe of the Cincinnati Astro-

The Ghoulardi All Stars, and did we have fun. Those really were the good old days. I'm second from left in the front row, next to Ernie "Ghoulardi" Anderson, and you can't miss "Big Chuck" Schodowski, standing on the left. Ernie claimed he convinced TV8 to hire me because, after seeing me play on the Channel 3 team, he wanted me on his team.

DICK'S MEMORIES

Ghoulardi

After KYW took me to Philadelphia with them in 1965, I soon grew homesick, even though the viewers there were very good to me. As it turned out, I was given offers from all three channels in Cleveland to return.

I loved baseball and survived a tryout with the Brooklyn Dodgers right out of high school. After playing well in a softball game for KYW against Ernie Anderson—Ghoulardi—and Channel 8, the rumor arose that Ghoulardi went to management at his station and told them to sign me to an "athletic scholarship." I have now been with Channel 8 for more than forty-five years.

I first met Ernie when I was standing near a bus stop on Euclid Avenue. Several elderly ladies were also waiting at the bus stop when Ghoulardi pulled up in a convertible driven by his girlfriend. After giving me his standard "Hi, Knif!" he pulled away, pulled out a water pistol, and sprayed the startled senior citizens.

Ghoulardi was literally one of a kind. I still have the memo from Channel 8 warning him not to ride his motorcycle through the station. His irate wife came into the station one evening and threw most of his clothing into the lobby.

nomical Observatory. The invention of the telegraph in the 1840s made a national weather service possible, but from the 1870s into the early 1920s the government forecasters were like a puppy chasing its tail when it came to getting the weather word out to the public.

Professor
Cleveland Abbe

Until the beginning of commercial radio, government weather forecasts were disseminated to the public using the U.S. mail, whistles, cannons, rockets, and bombs, and by hoisting flags of different colors. In Ohio, the forecast flags bore these symbols: full sun, crescent sun, and star, in either red or blue. In red, the full sun was a forecast of rising temperatures, the crescent sun foretold lower temperatures, and the star indicated steady temperatures. A blue sun warned of general rain or snow, a blue crescent sun presaged fair weather, and a blue star forecast localized rain or snow. An oncoming cold wave was depicted by an ominous black square in the middle of a six-by-eight-foot white flag. When winds of over 25 mph were expected, a red flag was unfurled. The forecast flags were hung from post offices and other buildings, while some trains were also adorned with the banners on their baggage cars.

This is someone I used to watch on Channel 8, long before I had any notion of being on television myself. It's Warren Guthrie, who was chairman of the speech department at Western Reserve University and broadcast as the "Sohio Reporter" on WJW from 1951 to 1963. He used only brief notes to deliver a 15-minute nightly newscast he wrote himself.

By 1901, weather service forecasts were being distributed by telegraph, telephone, and mail to about 80,000 customers. In 1904 some 60,000 farmers in Ohio were getting the daily weather forecast from Washington, D.C., by telephone within one hour of its issue. In 1939, New York City began its automatic telephone answering system, and within four days about 58,000 calls were being made daily.

Radio telegraphy started in 1914, and the commercial radio industry that followed revolutionized the business of dispensing weather information. While radio station KDKA in Pittsburgh, Pennsylvania, claims it was the first to broadcast a weather report, on April 26, 1921, it appears that E. B. Rideout of WEEI in Boston hit the airwaves with the first forecast in August 1920. For more than forty years Rideout's Yankee twang filled the New England air. By 1923, 140 radio stations across the country were broadcasting weather reports.

An interesting sidelight to the beginning of private weather forecasting was the professional jealousy of the government service. All weather forecasters in this country must rely on the same raw weather data provided by the National Weather Service headquartered in Washington, D.C. The animosity became so intense that in the 1930s and 1940s the government put up a vigorous fight to keep all the weather information for itself. The late Dr. Irving Krick, the iconoclastic proponent of long-range forecasting (whom I met a few years ago while doing a story on his involvement in forecasting for the Allies' D-day invasion in 1944), told me that the United States Weather Bureau shut off all of his teletypes at Caltech in 1938. This curious battle ended by the late 1940s, when the government was forced to recognize the entitlement of the private sector to information that is the result of taxpayer funding.

Cooperation is now the rule, but I'm sure that many government meteorologists look upon their blow-dried TV counterparts the way a golfer who shoots 105 looks down on someone who shoots 115.

Much credit for the surge in nationwide weather interest must go to the television enterprise known as The Weather Channel. TWC first glowed on cable screens at 8 p.m. on May 2, 1982. Two weather personalities very familiar to Northeast Ohioans appeared on that show: André Bernier, the ace morning forecaster on Fox 8, and the silky-smooth Bruce Edwards (Kalinowski), from Garfield Heights. TWC, which was the idea of Chicago meteorologist John Coleman, struggled mightily for its first five years and was close to bankruptcy (average annual losses of about $800,000 were sustained each of the first three years). Many television executives called The Weather Channel a laughingstock, but they underestimated its audience. TWC turned the corner by 1988, and in the 1990s it became a solid, profitable business. Initially seen in 3.2 million homes on cable service, by 1995 TWC was available in 52 million of the 61 million homes that subscribed to cable.

The first television weather presenter was "Wooly Lamb," a meteorologist in sheep's clothing. Wooly Lamb, a puppet, made his debut in limited-area viewing on NBC in New York City in

> *As long as the world shall last, there will be wrongs. If no man objected and no man rebelled, those wrongs would last forever.*
>
> —CLARENCE DARROW

HANG ON, HARRY... HERE COMES THE REVISED FORECAST!

DICK'S MEMORIES

Beloved Brillo Head

I envy people with curly hair. In my youth (I was young once) my mom told me that in order to have curly hair I had to eat the crust on my bread. (It didn't work, but I still have hair.) While on the news set with Tim Taylor and Robin Swoboda one evening, I saw a fly land on Tim's forehead. It went into his curls and was never seen again. I realized that Tim's hair was a condominium for flying insects. I also used Tim's hair as a humidity indicator. When his curls straightened, I knew that rain was on the way. Another benefit of working with Tim was that he gave me his old clothes. (He paid more for a tie than I did for my Higbee's sport coat.)

I always called him the Beloved Brillo Head.

I used to look up to him as the poor man's Walter Cronkite. One night the director came in during a break and said, "Taylor, Taylor, there's tanker spill," and started reading the names of all the chemicals, starting with hydrochloride. Taylor says, "We'll do the story, but leave the big words out." I said, "Wait a minute! Would Cronkite say, 'Leave the big words out'?"

If people only knew what went on during the commercial break. The night Tim said, "Goddard, I'm in no damn mood for your shenanigans," he came into the studio and there was a woman there with all her pets. They had been in a cage, but they got out as the red (on-air) light came on. As he's saying "Good evening, everyone," the cats climb up the screen behind the news desk. You knew Taylor was in trouble when he began to do his pigeon: "Ooh. Ooh." He did laugh about it, though—he does have a great sense of humor.

Millions long for immortality who do not know what to do with themselves on a rainy Sunday afternoon.

—SUSAN ERTZ

Jan's Judgment

Jan Jones has always been a favorite of mine. Pleasant and forever smiling. During a noon weather segment on Channel 5 she showed a visual of a dozen cattle lying on the ground in Stark County. She commented on how cute the scene was and how unusual to see so many cows sleeping. Off camera you could hear a voice say, "They're dead!" since they had been hit by lightning. "Oh," said Jan. "They're dead!"

October 1941. Wooly, who had a seven-year career and was sponsored by Botany Wrinkle-Proof Ties, would begin the report by looking into a telescope, then turn to the camera and sing the forecast. To cement the forecast in viewers' minds, Wooly would fade to black, and a slide would appear with the prophecy spelled out.

In the early days of TV weather, the airwaves were populated by puppets, magicians, and comedians (my first nasty letter was from a viewer whose main complaint was, "You're not funny!"). There were also well-endowed young ladies with names such as Sunny Day and Stormy Gale (who "simply love the weather"). The turn toward weatherpeople with meteorological training began in the late 1940s. The first credentialed weatherperson to gain national attention was Chicago's rotund Clint Youle, who was a regular on John Cameron Swayze's *Camel News Caravan* on NBC beginning in 1949. (I propose that there is a public preference for weathercasters who are pleasingly plump, with the large and lovable Willard Scott as the paradigm. Many of the panjandrums of prognostication are both personable and portly. The government should fund a study on this.)

By the 1960s, many major-market television stations began to hire forecasters who had been trained in meteorology, often with a background in the United States Air Force or Navy. The on-air time for weather broadcasts increased to two and three minutes. By the late 1970s, computer-graphics systems were generating colorful, glitzy, and sometimes animated maps and illustrations.

Jim Fidler—not to be confused with Hollywood columnist Jimmie Fidler, whose Tinseltown reports were heard on WHK radio into the 1960s—became Ohio's first television forecaster on WLWT Cincinnati. The station went on the air on Channel 5 a couple of months after Ohio's first TV station, WEWS in Cleveland. The station used the hyphen, calling itself WLW-T, with the T for television, to distinguish itself from its older radio sister, WLW. It's now simply WLW. Fidler also was the first weatherman on the *Today* show.

No one has ever lost money by underestimating the intelligence of the American public.

—H.L. MENCKEN

"HIM? HE HANDLES THE LONG-RANGE FORECASTS"

Jimmie Fidler became Ohio's first television forecaster on WLW Cincinnati in 1947. Fidler had begun his broadcast career on WLBC-AM radio in Muncie, Indiana, in 1934. The station billed him as "Radio's First Weatherman," which of course he was not. But the Museum of Television and Radio in New York credits him as being the first television weatherman because he gave a forecast for an experimental station in Cincinnati in 1940. And he was the first weatherman on the *Today* show when it debuted on NBC in 1952.

Those who have watched Cleveland weather programs over the years will fondly recall a number of favorites. After returning to Akron from the air force in 1955, I remember watching the good-humored and ebullient Joe Finan, dressed as a gas-station attendant in cap and bow tie, doing the weather as the Atlantic Weatherman on KYW. Jim Doney, the talented and affable host of the local travel program *Adventure Road* on WJW, doubled as the weekend weatherperson. I recall the night that Jim sent viewers into hysterics by taking nearly all of his allotted weather time trying to locate the state of Wyoming.

Some may remember the first weatherperson to offer scientific reasoning for why the forecast went wrong. Paul Annear, from Baldwin-Wallace College, was a mathematics professor who made a brief TV appearance around 1950.

When I started at KYW, my cross-town competitors were Carolyn Johnson on WEWS and the venerable Howard Hoffmann (the station's first announcer) on WJW. Hoolihan the Weatherman (Bob Wells) was a popular weather presenter at WJW in the 1960s and 1970s, while the versatile Don Webster began his weather career at WEWS in the early 1960s. Amiable Al Roker entertained viewers on WKYC from the late 1970s into the early 1980s before joining (and then replacing) his buddy, Willard Scott, on the *Today* show in New York.

As the 1990s drew to a close, the Fox 8 weather team of André Bernier, Mark Koontz, and Dick Goddard could claim the record for unit longevity.

Some of my fondest memories are from the early 1970s, when I was locked in television weather combat with two other

This was TV8's main anchor team of the early 1970s: Jim Hale, yours truly, Jeff Maynor and sportscaster Jim Mueller.

DICK'S PALS

Trying to Tame a Force of Nature

"BIG CHUCK" SCHODOWSKI: We used to have directors' meetings at the station to talk about various issues with news. One constant problem we had was Goddard running over on time with his weather segment, sometimes two minutes too long. I said, "The only way you're going to stop him is somebody has to cut him. What else can we do? We're screaming 'Wrap it up, wrap it up' for two minutes.

"You know what?" I continued, "I'm the only one here who can get away with it. I can cut him, and he'll get mad, but he won't do anything about it."

I usually directed weekends, but once in awhile I'd do weekdays. The next time I did, I told Dick, "I'm not used to doing weekdays, and I'm really nervous, so don't run long. If you do, we have to cut things, and cram, and it gets really hectic."

So I warned him. Dick is a good friend. He did the weather, I wrapped him up, and he went on. I started repeating in his earpiece, "Wrap it up, wrap it up, wrap it up." He kept talking. I said, "OK, stand by to roll commercial." Everybody in the control room looked at me in surprise. "Five seconds to roll," I said. "And roll it." Once you roll, you've got to take it on the air. Everybody in the control room had bug-eyed looks. Dick was in the middle of something, and the commercial came on. I figured I'd hear "About time somebody did that," but the control room was silent and no one would look at me. As soon as the news was over, everybody cleared out of the room as fast as they could.

Dick came over and looked in the door. I could see his reflection in the monitor, shaking his head. He'd call me Charlie when he was upset with me, because he knew I don't like it. He just said one word.

"Charlie," he said, sounding real disappointed.

The next three times I did the news, he was off as much as ten seconds early—"or Big Chuck's gonna cut me again," he said.

In a month or so, he was back to running over.

"Big Chuck" Schodowski was an award-winning producer and director at TV8 from 1960 to 2007, but is better known for collaborating with Ernie Anderson on Ghoulardi *and then hosting the* Hoolihan & Big Chuck *and* Big Chuck & Lil' John *shows—the longest local late-night run in TV history. He produced more than two thousand skits for the shows and is author of the memoir* Big Chuck!

I loved *The Mary Tyler Moore Show*, so it was a treat to join a skit with news director Lou Grant (Ed Asner, at the desk) and anchor Ted Baxter (Ted Knight, across from him) not long after the show started in 1970. Standing with me are TV8's *City Camera* news anchors at that time, Marty Ross and Murray Stewart.

ex–air force meteorologists: Bob Zames, an excellent forecaster, was at WEWS (ABC), while Herbert W. Kinnan was at WKYC (NBC).

Wally Kinnan was arguably the best weather forecaster ever to hit town. In World War II, Wally was in a P-38 Lightning that was shot down over Germany, and he spent time in a Nazi prisoner of war stalag. After his military career, Wally became a TV legend in Philadelphia. That lasted until 1965, when the Federal Communications Commission ordered the reversal of a station swap that NBC had engineered a decade earlier. Westinghouse and KYW went to Philadelphia, taking *The Mike Douglas Show* and a number of people, including me. NBC came back to Cleveland.

Wally Kinnan the Weatherman was the big guy in Philadelphia. He and the station's general manager were very good friends. He didn't really want to come to Cleveland, and I didn't really want to go to Philadelphia. I called him to talk about it, and we might never have made the switch, but he was on vacation and never called back.

I was in Philadelphia starting the first day of summer 1965. I liked it, but I didn't know anybody there. I didn't care if it rained. I was on the air three months there. The volume of mail was wonderful; I had a great reception, but I wanted to come home. I was still married, my mom and dad were still alive, and everything was still back in Akron. I wanted to come home.

DICK'S MEMORIES

Bell Bottom

Doug Adair would sit on a phone book to be higher behind the anchor desk. He wore white pants one day, and evidently the ink hadn't solidified. So on the back of Doug's pants he had "Ohio Bell" written backwards. I said, "Doug, if you're going to advertise and get paid, you better flip it over!"

Here's one from the KYW-TV days, probably from the Saturday morning *Barn-Wood Playhouse*. From left are Woodrow the Woodsman (Clay Conroy), straw-hatted Barnaby (Linn Sheldon), one of Barnaby's "little neighbors," and KYW radio disc jockey Jim Runyon, who was known a few years later as the narrator of radio's "Chickenman" series. (Cleveland Press Collection, Cleveland State University Archives)

They never signed me to a contract, and I had offers in Cleveland from KYW, WEWS, and WJW. So I resigned and came back home. I'm a sports nut, and back in those days Channel 8 did the Browns games, which played a big part in my going to the station—although Ernie Anderson always claimed he got the station to hire me so I could play for his Ghoulardi All-Stars.

Wally and I became friendly competitors. I admired him for many reasons, and one of them was that he didn't suffer weather fools gladly. A major cross-country bus company sponsored his evening weathercast in Philadelphia, and a viewer had sent Wally an especially venomous letter criticizing his forecasting skills. Wally read the letter on the air and responded by telling his new pen pal that he would like to see him under the next bus leaving Philadelphia. And Wally was put into high dudgeon when a non-meteorologist competitor who couldn't qualify for the AMS Seal of Approval decided to create and display his own fancy Shield of Approval.

Nothing says more about the character of a man than the things he makes fun of.

—GOETHE

I'm in the upper right of this singing Christmas promotion featuring KYW TV and radio personalities about 1964. Also included in this photo are Mike Douglas (front row, left), "world's handsomest disc jockey" Jerry G. Bishop (second to left), and Barnaby (Linn Sheldon—center). (Cleveland Press Collection, Cleveland State University Archives)

One day when Wally and I were laughin', scratchin', and tellin' lies around the golf course, I accused him of being a meteorological Typhoid Mary for bringing the five-day forecast with him from Philadelphia. Wally shot back that since his evening weather show was about two minutes ahead of mine, I should assign an intern to copy his forecast for me.

At least Wally and I are proof that being telegenic is not a requirement for some measure of television longevity.

Wally's gone now, but the extended forecasts are still with us and getting longer. They're just ridiculous. The longer one goes, the less accurate it's going to be. I used to do a three-day forecast. Wally made it five, and now we do eight, because we're Fox 8.

Thank goodness we're not Channel 19.

WORDS ON WAR

A Glimpse of Hell

Patriotism is supporting your country all the time and your government when it deserves it.

—Mark Twain

As my military career was coming to a close, I was with the United States Air Force Task Group during Operation Castle on Enewetak (then Eniwetok) Atoll in the Marshall Islands of the western Pacific Ocean. Enewetak is 2,700 miles southwest of the Hawaiian Islands in the part of the Pacific Ocean known as Micronesia.

Atolls are clusters of tiny coral islands that ride in the deep blue Pacific, caressed by the soothing northeast trade winds and washed in warm sunshine. The cerulean skies are dotted with small, cottony cumulus clouds, a few of which can be relied upon to provide a brief and refreshing tropical rain shower at about two o'clock every afternoon. With the steady sunshine, gentle winds, and high temperatures around 80 degrees, I had found a heaven on earth.

It was there that I caught a glimpse of hell.

JOINT TASK FORCE SEVEN

CERTIFICATE OF ACHIEVEMENT

FOR MERITORIOUS SERVICE IN CONNECTION WITH ATOMIC ENERGY TESTS AT ENIWETOK-BIKINI

OPERATION CASTLE

1954

PRESENTED TO: A/1c Richard D. Goddard

I was part of a group of six meteorologists who gave weather support for the detonation of a hydrogen bomb in the Pacific on March 1, 1954.

Education's purpose is to replace an empty mind with an open one.

—MALCOLM S. FORBES

On March 1, 1954, at 5:55 a.m., I peered, along with half a dozen other air force meteorologists, into the predawn pitch blackness toward the atoll of Bikini, some 175 miles to the east. We were hoping to see at least a faint glimmer from the world's first full-yield hydrogen bomb detonation.

Suddenly, at H-hour, the sky to the east blossomed into the brightest high noon of summer. I'm sure that none of us could testify to the ultimate brilliance since we turned in unison away from the dazzling flash and covered our eyes with our hands. Within seconds the blinding glow from the false sun faded into the prebomb blackness. There was no sound, save for the lapping of the water in the lagoon.

We had calculated that it would take about thirteen minutes for the sound wave to travel the 175 miles from Bikini to Enewetak. I can't recall that any of us spoke during the endless wait for the sound of the H-bomb.

The best way to destroy an enemy is to make him a friend.

—ANONYMOUS

When the sound arrived, it was not the thunderous rumbling that one might expect from such a cataclysmic explosion. Instead, it more resembled the sharp crack from a rifle held close to the ear.

Those who had been on atomic tests the years before were even more stunned than those of us new to the project. Never before had Bikini detonations been visible on Enewetak. Even the first attempt at nuclear fusion of an H-bomb, Operation Ivy, on November 1, 1952, was not visible over such a great distance. Unbeknown, the first H-bomb had been a dud.

Several days after the H-bomb detonation, we flew over Bikini Atoll. On the flight we passed over numerous islets whose palm trees had been leveled by previous atomic blasts. It was an incredible sight, since the palm trees had all been felled in the same direction and seemed to point, like fingers of the dead, toward the terrible thing that had killed them.

Finally, we arrived over ground zero. Below us, where a few days before there had been a small coral island shimmering in the tropical sun, there was now only a large and very dark blue circle of water. The tiny island had vaporized.

I recalled seeing Dr. Edward Teller, the bushy-browed physicist known as the Father of the H-Bomb, in the weather office a few days before the blast. I wondered what this seemingly kind man now felt about his terrible stepchild.

Today, with H-bombs in the multi-megaton range, the March 1, 1954, device would be puny by comparison. We can only pray and work to ensure that man, the deadliest of all animals, will harness not only nuclear power, but himself as well.

This is a rare shot—me with my hair out of place. But giving a thumbs up after flying with the Air Force Thunderbirds in an F-16 Fighting Falcon.

Raising Hackles

War does not decide who is right, only who is left.

—Bertrand Russell

The worst sin towards our fellow creatures is not to hate them but to be indifferent to them. That is the essence of inhumanity.

—GEORGE BERNARD SHAW

I believe that this nation is the greatest of all on this small, rocky planet. For four years I served my beloved country, and I would do it again if I could. I also believe that through our government's arrogance and imagined moral supremacy we have lost our way and have earned the hatred of many of our fellow human beings.

We had the sympathy of the world following the terrorist attacks on 9/11. But, because of our government's reckless and insouciant attitude, we have again embarked on a war that never should have been fought. We had the respect of the free world following our success against Adolf Hitler and his insane conspirators. Many of our leaders who took us into the wars in Korea and Vietnam have, in retrospect, publicly admitted that both were "mistakes."

*   *   *

Those who glorify war are inhuman zealots. Our latest venture into an unending conflict has claimed the lives of thousands of brave men and women. The current war will eventually top three trillion dollars, and it has hastened this nation's downward economic spiral. Why we invade countries that have been killing each other for centuries over religious differences is absurd.

The only event that could unite mankind is the threat of an alien invasion. In order to navigate the universe, the aliens would need to have such supreme intelligence that they would have nothing to do with us.

I wouldn't worry.

Happy Trails Animal Sanctuary cares for many abused farm animals, such as horses, chickens, ducks, and even potbelly pigs.

If you have no regrets, you need to get out more often.

In the spring of 2010, I attended an ROTC graduation at my alma mater, Kent State University. I'm wearing my original U.S. Air Force uniform—shade 84 blue, and it still fits. I told them I qualified as a sharpshooter but hate guns, and I talked about the last three wars, which should never have been fought.

WEATHER OFFICE

(Cleveland Press Collection, Cleveland State University Archives)

DICK'S PALS

The person who says he never makes mistakes usually does not make anything.

Making a Big Exit

TIM TAYLOR: We went to dinner between news shows one evening. It was either a pizza joint or Chinese, the other favorite. As Dick is leaving, he's always working the crowd: "Here's a woolly bear," "Oh, mostly cloudy," "How's the weather gonna be?"—using the lines I've heard a million times. He's backing out, as always, never watching where he's going. I'm almost out the door, and I notice as he's backing out that right next to the door there's another door—which, it turns out, was a closet. Dick opens the door and he goes into the closet. To avoid embarrassment, once he realizes where he is—and I'm watching this—he stays in there. He exits a few seconds later, with a wave, going, "Yeah, it was good to see you, OK," as though it was an office. You couldn't make this stuff up.

Fast Food

ROBIN SWOBODA: We used to go to dinner a lot—fast food. Dick and I got to Taco Bell one night and got two orders of nachos, one for me and one for Tim. We pulled into the parking lot and one spilled out. I picked them up, put them back in the bag, and Dick said, "Those are Tim's." I said no, they'd be mine, I dropped them. He said, "No, Robby, I've had pizzas fly out of the box and picked them up. If he's not going to go for the food, what he doesn't know won't hurt him."

Tim had a kidney stone not long after that. I said, "Maybe it's gravel."

No Cheering in the Press Box

TIM TAYLOR: The station sent Robin and Goddard and me to Atlanta in 1995 when the Indians were in the World Series. We did our shows from there. It was a very big deal, and we had a ball. Channel 5 was there, too, and Dick would walk into their live shots. We sat in the press box during the games. Kenny Lofton in the first game stole first and stole second, and Goddard was going nuts, cheering in the press box. We were also guilty, I'll admit. The PA announcer comes on and says, "We must caution those in the press box. It is inappropriate to cheer—you are members of the media." We all slithered down in our seats. Dick says, "That wasn't me; that was Robin and Tim."

Robin always kept smiling, even when cats pooped under the news desk. ("And they had worms," she pointed out.)

"TONIGHT'S HEAVY SNOW WARNING IS CANCELED DUE TO LACK OF INTEREST"

What Are You Afraid Of?

To conquer fear is the beginning of wisdom.

—Bertrand Russell

· ·

Neeeding only a few hours' credit before graduation, I enrolled in Psychology 101. The professor was physically impressive, a woman with the dimensions of a medium-sized dray horse and an unkempt hairstyle that reminded one of the Gorgon Medusa. When she was in high dudgeon, which, as it turned out, was quite often, she was a daunting presence.

And she was a wonderful teacher. There was no dozing off in Psych 101.

Her special interest was in the study of phobias, defined as morbid, irrational, or excessive fears of particular objects or endeavors. (I was soon stricken with flunkophobia.)

I recall being told that humans are born with only two natural fears: the fear of heights and the fear of loud noises. All other trepidations are cultural, picked up from parents, siblings, friends, and others. It's difficult to believe that anyone can escape phobias. You can bet that if you have an excessive fear, there's a scientific name for it. You can also be assured that you are in good company.

Like so many of the world's powerful military and political leaders, Julius Caesar and Napoleon Bonaparte feared cats (ailurophobia). Both Fox sports announcer John Mad-

No matter how much cats fight there always seems to be plenty of kittens.

—ABRAHAM LINCOLN

"...AND A LXV PERCENT CHANCE OF THUNDERSTORMS TODAY, DECREASING TO XX PERCENT TOMORROW."

"STAY COOL, DUDE. THEY CAN SENSE FEAR."

The reason a dog has so many friends is that he wags his tail instead of his tongue.

den and renowned sci-fi writer Ray Bradbury chose to travel by bus due to fear of flying (aerophobia). Author Graham Greene admitted to two mental aberrations: fear of birds (ornithophobia) and blood (hematophobia). Glenallen Hill, the former Cleveland Indians outfielder, suffers from arachnophobia, the dread of spiders. While Hill was with the Toronto Blue Jays, he once dreamed of spiders, jumped out of bed, and injured his leg so badly that he went on the fifteen-day disabled list.

If you plan a career in meteorology, you should be free from the following aversions: chionophobia (snow), nephophobia (clouds), ombrophobia (rain), anemophobia (wind), heliophobia (sunlight), cheimaphobia (cold), homichlophobia (fog), and hydrophobia (water).

Potential astronomers can bag it if they have an aversion to the moon (selenophobia), stars (siderophobia), or to dawn (eosophobia).

Those in the medical profession have taken the proverbial two strikes if they have these roadblocks: bacteriophobia (germs), gymnophobia (nakedness), nosemaphobia (illness), mysophobia (infection), and kopophobia (physical examination). At least two, however, could be an occasional ally: hynophobia (sleep) and cathisophobia (sitting down).

One of the most famous phobias is the fear of the number 13, triskaidekaphobia. One of the most esoteric has to be arachibutyrophobia. (Just in case you're wondering, that's the fear of having peanut butter stick to the roof of your mouth—honest.) Pity those who suffer polyphobia (fear of many things), but have even more compassion for those with panophobia (fear of everything). It was President Franklin Delano Roosevelt who told us "the only thing we have to fear is fear itself!" That would be phobophobia.

The Roman emperor Tiberius endured keraunophobia, the dread of thunderstorms. Tiberius called upon his scribes and soothsayers to protect him from thunderbolts that were occasionally thrown his way by the great god Jupiter. Someone offered the observation that the laurel bush was never struck by lightning, so a garland of laurel leaves was made and placed upon the emperor's brow. From that day forward, Roman emperors wore a wreath of laurel leaves.

As a rule, man's a fool, always wanting what it's not.
When it's hot he wants it cool, when it's cool he wants it hot.

True Lies

A lie can travel halfway around the world
while truth is putting on its shoes.

—Mark Twain

This masked marvel joining me at the weather board at Channel 3 in 1963 was a fellow known only as the Tulsa Rainmaker. He claimed he could make it rain in Tulsa within 72 hours of any specified day and time, and three times made good on it, despite predictions of no rain by the local U.S. Weather Bureau office. One reason he kept his identity secret was that he was sued after the third storm produced flooding and set a Tulsa record of 9 inches of rain in 24 hours. He enjoyed brief national notoriety and never did unmask himself.

Three decades of research by psychologists in the United States have suggested that men lie more often than women. (Could men who fish have skewed the results?) But the percentage difference is narrowing. A 1980 study of "who lies more often" concluded that males lied ten times more often than females. The most recent study, however, suggests that men now lie only three times as often as women. (Way to go, girls!)

Psychologists have also determined that the classic accepted sign that someone is lying does not exist: Liars do not avert their eyes; they gaze directly and unblinkingly at you.

While there is no one trait that reveals a Pinocchio among us, liars often move their arms, hands, and fingers much less than those who are telling the truth. A liar's voice will frequently become more high-pitched and strained, along with obvious pauses in their storytelling. This indicates a need to concentrate on their fibs.

According to psychologists, most people tell at least one lie during every ten minutes of conversation. Many of these untruths must be in the "little white lie" category, such as the almost automatic reply of "good" in response to the ubiquitous Jersey Guy's witty "How ya' doin'?"

The lies, whether white or any other color, are programmed into humans in childhood. Specialists in child behavior estimate that by age two and a half, 65 percent of children lie . . . and they do it well.

A liar's voice will frequently become more high-pitched and strained.

He is your friend, your partner, your defender, your dog. You are his life, his love, his leader. He will be yours, faithful and true, to the last beat of his heart. You owe it to him to be worthy of such devotion.

Seldom are the little con artists reprimanded, so they quickly learn it's not a big deal. Experts tell parents that this is wrong. They should not let the tykes off the hook. Researchers also tell us that the higher a child's IQ, the more likely he or she is to fib.

There is a difference in what females and males lie about. Women often lie to protect the feelings of others, or to protect the macho male's fragile ego. (I recently saw a woman in Cleveland driving by with an Ohio license plate that read: MEN LIE.)

Men frequently lie to boost their self-esteem. As an example, the majority of male golfers never break 100, but they often report their score using the Celsius scale.

While both sexes cheat in their relationships, men are the leaders in marital indiscretions. Women, however, are trying their best to catch up in illicit affairs. According to one estimate, there has been a 50 percent increase in female infidelity in the last decade.

As you can imagine, trying to find the truth about lying isn't easy (and that's the truth). But how about that modern technological marvel called the "lie detector," or polygraph? The courts have decided—in spite of protests from those who manufacture the devices—that polygraphs are unreliable, and their results are not admissible in most states.

Polygraphs measure respiration (breathing), blood pressure, and pulse rate. As scientific as it is purported to be, the lie detector is only as accurate as the machine's operator says it is.

In terms of litigation, lies fall into two categories: libel and slander. Both relate to false statements that can injure a person's good name and reputation. While libel can refer to something expressed either orally or in writing, slander is confined to the spoken word (although scripted words spoken in a movie or television program are usually interpreted by the courts as being libelous, since they are more lasting than ordinary speech).

TV8's *City Camera* news team lines up for a promotional shot in 1967. From left are sportscaster Frank Glieber, news anchors Doug Adair and Marty Ross, and me.

Stats

I started doing stats for the Cleveland Browns in 1966, when TV8 was a CBS affiliate and the NFL had local stations doing the games. Channel 8 was doing the Browns. When I came back from Philadelphia, in fact, I had offers from all three stations—3, 5, and 8—and I thought, by golly, I'm going with the station that does the Browns. That's what won me over.

Our sports anchor, Frank Glieber, called the games on TV. He came to the station one day and said, "Goddard, I know you really like football. Would you like to do stats?" And that was it. After Frank was let go, Gib Shanley asked if I would like to do the radio stats for him and my TV3 pal Jim Graner, who did the color. I've been doing it ever since. I flew with the team for a couple of years, but I just do home games now.

I put up boards on the wall that I mark with a grease pencil. I just do offense or make notes of any other play of consequence. I wipe out a number and update with the grease pencil how many times the ball has been carried, the yards gained, and first downs. And I keep track of what anybody on offense has done. You get to be the proverbial one-armed paper hanger. I hate Indianapolis and Cincinnati—they run series and you have no chance to keep up.

Thank goodness, as the season wears on, they have a little heater they put under the counter. Our feet were warm, but they do take the windows out in the broadcast booth where we work. I'll never forget the time I came back from a Hawaii tour for what became the famous Red Right 88 playoff game in January 1981. It was about 85 degrees when we left Honolulu. The next morning the wind chill in the stadium was about 35 below zero. That was incredible.

Jim Brown is arguably the greatest football player ever. He left the game before I started doing stats, but I saw his first game with the Cleveland Browns in 1957 against the Pittsburgh Steelers in the annual preseason game at the Akron Rubber Bowl. And I met up with Jim at a recent Browns game, in the long corridor that leads to the press box elevator. Jim was limping on both legs, and I was limping on my right leg from a knee replacement. We were talking as we went, and as we neared the yellow line in front of the elevator, I thought, wait a minute—this is the chance of a lifetime!

I hobbled ahead and made sure that I stepped over the line first. I had beaten the football legend in a foot race. It helped that Jim didn't realize he was in a limp-off.

It's been my experience that people who have no vices have very few virtues.

—ABRAHAM LINCOLN

THE
OHIO COUNTRY MYTH

No one knows how the Ohio Country Myth was born, but flowing tankards of ale on cruel, frigid winter nights in New England no doubt played a large part in fueling the wild speculation.

It was the late 1700s, and the intriguing story was that just over the snow-covered mountains west of New England lay a bountiful land of milk and honey with weather so mild and benevolent that ice and frost were almost total strangers. This eighteenth-century version of Camelot was known as Ohio Country, and the land was there for those who were ambitious and adventurous enough to pack up and claim it for a modest fee. The goal of those who decided to take on the challenge was, basically, quick wealth. How could they go wrong in an uncharted land where, it was rumored, "plants yielded ready-made candles and trees spontaneously produced sugar"?

One brochure describing the Ohio Country read as follows: "A climate wholesome and delightful with frost even in winter almost entirely unknown, and a river called, by way of eminence, the beautiful, and abounding in excellent fish of vast size. Venison in plenty, the pursuit of which is uninterrupted by wolves, foxes, lions, or tigers. A couple of swine will multiply themselves a hundred-fold in two years without taking any care of them."

Unfortunately, it didn't take long for those who crossed the Appalachian Mountains to the Ohio Country to be disabused of their optimism. Somehow overlooked in the glowing prospectus was the imminent danger of attack by Indians along with the threat of injury or death from an assortment of crawl-

THOU KNOWEST THOU CAN TRUST OUR KING ARTHUR ACCOUNTANTS!

It is not the years in your life but the life in your years that counts.

—ADLAI STEVENSON

ing and leaping indigenous creatures (I will grant that—to my knowledge—free-roaming lions have never been a problem in Ohio).

The plentiful wildlife included the much-feared cougar, plus deer, bear, elk, beaver, muskrat, and turkey. The raccoon was a favored hunting target and food source for both the Indians and settlers. This clever animal with its bandit's mask is still abundant in Ohio, as our tipped-over garbage cans demonstrate. Ohio's Geauga County was named for this mammal (the Indian name for raccoon being "sheauga").

Other creatures the Ohio Country pioneers faced were poisonous serpents. Copperhead snakes abounded, with their nasty penchant for living near human dwellings. Rattlesnakes pervaded the Lake Erie islands north of Sandusky, basking on lily pads in the shimmering summer sunshine. Trappers warned others not to set foot on the islands.

To the early settlers' dismay, Ohio winters were just as harsh and snowy as those in New England. Often, more so. But there certainly was an abundance of flora and fauna. The Ohio Country in the 1700s was 95 percent forest. It would have been possible for an imaginative and agile squirrel to climb a tree along the Lake Erie shore and travel all the way to the Ohio River without touching the ground.

Other creatures the Ohio pioneers faced were poisonous serpents.

Happiness is a warm woollybear—or in this case, four of them.

Every autumn thousands of friends, both bi- and quadruped, make a visit Vermilion, Ohio, for the Annual Woollybear Festival. (Katy McElroy, *Vermilion Photo Journal*)

Since trees return a tremendous amount of water to the air via a process called transpiration (a large oak tree can contribute fifty gallons each day), Ohio summers in those days must have been incredibly humid. The rising moisture in the atmosphere would have also fomented rain and thunderstorms (the legendary Burlington tornado of 1825 wiped out whole forests and may have been the strongest twister ever to strike Ohio). Add malaria, yellow fever, cholera, and dysentery to the litany of problems, and you can understand why the Ohio Country Myth was called by one early naturalist "a vulgar error."

In the 1700s the Ohio Country was home to a number of Indian tribes, and most were hostile to the invaders from the east. The Shawnee of southern Ohio, led by their great chief, Tecumseh, were particularly forceful in delaying the settlers' advance. The northeast portion of the Ohio territory was part of an Indian no-man's land; the Erie tribe had been all but annihilated in 1655 by their cousins to the east, the five-nation confederation known as the Iroquois.

Defying the prospect of Indian attacks, the first permanent settlement in Ohio was established in Marietta, in the extreme southeastern portion of the state, in April 1788. These pioneers were primarily from Massachusetts, and they called their organization the Ohio Land Company. Concurrently, the state of Connecticut had domain over a large portion of Ohio territory that it named the Western Reserve—in essence, New Connecticut. The extreme portion of the claimed land was designated the Firelands (it now comprises Erie and Huron counties). In 1775, thirty-five investors had subscribed to form the Connecticut Land Company, and three million acres of the Western Reserve were purchased for about forty cents an acre. The person chosen to lead entrepreneurs to the Promised Land was a prominent attorney from Canterbury, Connecticut, named Moses Cleaveland. Cleaveland, a Yale graduate, had served in the Revolutionary War and at the time was general of the Connecticut militia.

Time wounds all heels.

Described as swarthy and robust, Cleaveland led a fifty-man surveying and plotting party along the Lake Erie shore in July 1796, searching for the mouth of the river the Indians called "crooked water"—the Cuyahoga. On the steamy twenty-second day of the month, Cleaveland and his crew reached their goal, then spent the next three months chopping and hacking, carving out townships that were five miles square.

Moses Cleaveland and his surveyors never intended to settle in the Western Reserve, yearning to return to the comforts of New England. After a few months they returned to Connecticut, and Cleaveland died at the village of Wyndham in 1806 (three years after Ohio became a state). He never saw the success of the town that was named after him. (The story goes that the letter A was dropped from Cleaveland's name in a newspaper story of the time—and that, too, never returned.)

In retrospect, the name Carterland would have been more fitting for the settlement, since it was Lorenzo Carter and his wife who decided to stay and tough it out on the shores of Lake Erie. The Carter home became the town meeting place, and Carter welcomed new arrivals while imposing a modicum of law.

In 1800, Cleveland's population was seven; by 1810 it had reached fifty-seven. By 1820, with the Ohio and Erie Canals open and access gained to Lake Erie, the population had grown to 606, with fifty houses. In 1826, with 9,000, Cleveland was incorporated as a city.

Cleveland's population peaked in 1940 at over 900,000, while the 2000 census put our citizenry at 478,403. By 2009, according to the U.S. Census Bureau, it was 431,363.

> *One of the secrets of life is that all that is really worth doing is what we do for others.*
>
> —LEWIS CARROLL

DICK'S MEMORIES

Snoopy

Mark Koontz was on the air doing the weather. Our art director had a large schnauzer named Oliver. Oliver was occasionally brought into the station, and this day he managed to get through the studio doors. Oliver immediately went over to Mark and buried his nose in a very sensitive area. Very distracting. I figured that Mark deserved some sort of Emmy for trying to fight off Oliver with one hand while pointing to the weather map with the other.

DICK'S PALS

Creating Chaos and Loving It

TIM TAYLOR: Freddy McLeod, who does the Cavs games now, worked for us doing sports around 1980. Typical of sports guys back then, Freddy was prone to wear garish outfits. This one night he wore a maroon suit and leather boots with Cuban heels. Everyone was on the set at the beginning of the news. You'd get the four-shot, and then the weather and sports guys would leave.

The lead story I was reading was about a jogger who had been hit by a car right outside our studios on South Marginal. We go to video. Freddy jumps out of his seat and hits the freshly waxed floor at exactly the time I am saying the jogger was hit and propelled through the air. Freddy flies up in front of me, even with the riser we're sitting on, perpendicular to the floor, and lands on his back. There was a huge crash.

Goddard rushes over, waves like an umpire, and at the top of his lungs goes, "Safe!"

My inner thighs were black and blue by the end of that show, I was pinching myself so hard. I don't know how I got through it. That's one of many things he did to me on the air.

We used to show his always unpredictable cats or dogs up for adoption right on the news desk, until one too many "accidents" made it difficult for us to do the rest of the show without gagging.

He had kittens that got loose at the beginning of the show one night, and as I'm reading a serious lead story, these kittens are crawling up our legs and scratching. Mama cat is loose, too, and she is nervous and dropping mementos all over the set. Dick is on all fours under us, trying to collect them and just reveling in it, loving it.

He was telling viewers about a great cat one night, and the poor little guy suffered intestinal problems. While we tried valiantly to maintain some dignity, the equally unpredictable Robin accurately pointed out, "Oh my gosh, he has worms!"

> I love sports. I had four letters in high school and played baseball, football, and other sports as part of the Ghoulardi All-Stars at WJW.

It wasn't easy to finish that show. I think that's when management decided to start taping the animal segment in another studio.

He loved to hang in the studio, just waiting for something to go wrong so he could pounce and make it worse. Finally we actually banned him from the studio until his weather time because he created such chaos in there.

But of all the most inappropriate things he's ever done during a live newscast, this one defies any logic. You would swear it was made up and could never have happened. We were throwing to a live shot in Akron. I don't remember the exact story or wording, but it had to do with Tom Sawyer, the former mayor and congressman. We turned to the monitor in the middle of the news desk, and I started to ask a question—"Did Tom Sawyer . . ."—and that's all I got out of my mouth. Because at that point, during a live newscast, at the top of his lungs, Dick said, "No, but Huck Finn did!"

Everybody in the studio was like, "What just happened?" It was so bizarre. We went over the tape later. It's hard to pick stuff up if you're not directly on mic, but this was like a bomb. "No, but Huck Finn did!"

Dick said, "I didn't know you were live." The news was between 6 o'clock and 6:30, and this was maybe at 6:03 p.m. Management was mad, but that was part of the package. You couldn't do anything. They'd say, "Dick, don't go in there anymore," and it was like telling a kid, "Don't go in your brother's room."

After the show he'd look like Peck's Bad Boy and just be laughing.

> *Nature is neither kind nor cruel. Nature is indifferent.*
>
> —CHARLES DARWIN

> *Educating the mind without educating the heart is no education at all.*
>
> —ARISTOTLE

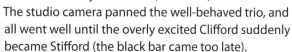

DICK'S MEMORIES

Sir Stifford

Wilma Smith brought her three beagles into the news studio one evening and introduced them to the audience individually: Cassandra, Clarence, and Clifford. The studio camera panned the well-behaved trio, and all went well until the overly excited Clifford suddenly became Stifford (the black bar came too late).

GO BUCKS!

The happiest people in the world are those who always manage to give without remembering, and to take without forgetting.

—SAMARITAN CREED

Ohio is known as the Buckeye State, and the nickname was likely born on September 2, 1788. It was on that date that Colonel Ebenezer Sproat, representing the United States government, met with American Indians in the part of Ohio that was then known as the Northwest Territory.

The Indians greeted Colonel Sproat with cries of "Hetuck, hetuck, hetuck." The word *hetuck* was Indian for "eye of the buck," and it was taken as a compliment since deer were a very important food source for the nature-dependent tribes.

An ashy-gray tree with scaly bark was found throughout the Northwest Territory, and since the fruit (seeds) that appeared on the tree in autumn resembled the eye of a male deer, it was logical to name the tree "buckeye."

It wasn't until 1840, however, that Ohio became recognized nationally as the Buckeye State. The notoriety came when presidential candidate William Henry Harrison used a log cabin made from buckeye wood as part of his campaign tactics. The image of a rough-and-ready president who lived in a log cabin (he didn't) and drank hard cider (he did) proved so appealing to the common folk that Harrison won election in a landslide over Martin Van Buren.

Ohio's state flag, which was created in 1902, features a red orb inside a white circle, which represents a buck's eye and the letter O. It was not until 1953, however, the "Buckeye State" became Ohio's official nickname.

The buckeye tree displays flowers at the ends of branches in spring. During summer, five elliptical leaflets are attached

"WE WOULD LIKE TO THANK W.K. FOR BRINGING THAT TO OUR ATTENTION."

to each stalk at a single point. In autumn the leaves take on a showy orange to yellow-brown color. My aunt's buckeye tree, next to Buchtel High School in Akron, has grown to an impressive and symmetrical 35 feet. Some buckeye trees can tower to 70 feet.

In summer the tree seeds are enclosed in a brownish-green pod that will split open in autumn to reveal one to three seeds (nuts) that, like a male deer's eye, are shiny and dark brown with one large tan spot. Unfortunately, the buckeye nuts—along with the tree's early leaves—are poisonous (crush a seed or twig, and you'll experience a foul odor). American Indians would mash the seeds and twigs and spread the material on lakes and ponds in order to stun fish and make them easy pickings (literally). Don't think about trying this today, since it is illegal in Ohio.

Buckeye wood has been used for log cabins, furniture, flooring, and musical instruments. Pioneers believed that carrying a buckeye nut in your pocket would ward off the pain of rheumatism.

Brutus Buckeye is the mascot of the Ohio State University sports teams. Brutus is very familiar to fans of the University of Michigan, but the only pain that the Maize and Blue occasionally feel is centralized in a lower part of the anatomy.

Left: The boys from Akron. One stayed, one left. He's a good guy, but I wish he'd do more for animals.

Right: Jerry Springer, the TV ringmaster and former Cincinnati politician, was the proud recipient of a woollybear sticker when he emceed the local Emmy show for the Cleveland chapter of the National Academy of Television Arts & Sciences in 1998.

DICK'S FANS

Tim Lones of Canton is one of Northeast Ohio's most knowledgeable viewers as writer and proprietor of the Cleveland Classic Media blog, at clevelandclassicmedia.blogspot.com.

Rich Tenaglia of Westlake is a longtime West Sider.

If you get to thinking you're a person of some influence, try ordering somebody else's dog around.

—WILL ROGERS

Easy to Relate To

TIM LONES: Dick has always taken his weather forecasting seriously. There is always a sense of fun and enjoyment in his voice. He's very easy to relate to. I've only met him once in person, but he was very easygoing—just like his on-air persona. Dick is from the Akron area (Green, to be exact), but unlike a certain athlete who was born in Akron, he never felt the need to "take his talents" to New York, Chicago, Los Angeles, or another bigger market. Dick will always be Cleveland's Own to us, and for fifty years, local viewers have been the better for it.

A Pizza for Dick

RICH TENAGLIA: I wanted to meet Dick Goddard and never did because of the weather, which I thought was ironic.

When I was a lad of sixteen, I worked in a pizza shop in Rocky River, not far from where he lived at the time. I was a dishwasher, earning my stripes to be a pizza maker. It was about time for me to go home one Sunday evening. I answered the phone and the guy says, "This is Dick Goddard," and he ordered a pizza. I said, "Spell that last name." He said, "G-o-d-d-a-r-d." I said, "Yeah, right. Who is this?" and the guy said, "Dick Goddard."

I told the owner that a guy claiming to be Dick Goddard ordered a pizza. "Oh sure," the owner said, "he's a regular customer." He'd been teaching me, so I said, "Let me make his pizza. I'll make a real nice one."

He supervised and I made it. It was around eight o'clock when Dick called, and I knocked around to nine, waiting for him to pick up. I waited until about quarter to ten, wondered what happened, and left. What happened was, between the time he called and the time I left, it seemed like about ten inches of snow fell. The roads were thoroughly covered, and driving was slow.

Dick did come in eventually, but I missed my chance. I hope he enjoyed the pizza!

Baseball legend Pete Rose isn't in the Hall of Fame, but I gave him a woollybear sticker when he came to town—always my highest tribute. (Janet Macoska)

Snowbelt Diary

September

It was late in the month when we arrived in Geauga County. We had traded the red clay of Georgia for the lush greenery of Northeast Ohio. It was a chlorophyll paradise that reminded us of the scene from *The Wizard of Oz,* when Dorothy and Toto first saw the Emerald City. We knew we weren't in Georgia anymore. What an exhilarating experience.

Some of the trees had already begun to show brilliant shades of red, orange, and bronze. Agnes and the girls raked the fallen leaves into huge piles, and they laughed uncontrollably as our West Highland terrier, Fluffkins, dove in and out of the leaves.

October

Folks around here told us that the first snowflakes would arrive before the month was over. More excitement, since the ladies had never seen snow before.

It was during the third week that we were awakened by the clatter of snow grains and snow pellets. We knew that the long-awaited snowflakes were on the way. Sure enough, here they came! The delicate flakes looked like lace doilies as they decorated the yard. Fluffy tried to catch them in her mouth. Ha ha. Hilarious.

We were disappointed that only about an inch of snow had accumulated. Two days later we were treated to an honest-to-goodness Lake Erie snow

April hath put a spirit of youth in everything.

—WILLIAM SHAKESPEARE

*All knowledge, the
totality of all questions
and all answers, is
contained in the dog.*

—FRANZ KAFKA

squall. In a short time the landscape began to look like a Currier & Ives post-card. This was more like it!

So Christmas came early for us.

November

In anticipation of the glorious Christmas holidays just ahead, our neighbors had created a lovely manger scene, complete with three wise men. How touching.

Snow had become an almost daily event by early month, and occasional freezing drizzle had created a skating rink in our driveway. Agnes slipped on the icy parfait, and by the time I had shoveled our way out, over an hour had passed before I got her to the emergency room at the hospital. The novelty of snow was beginning to wear off. Ha.

The snow had become so heavy that Fluffkins, our all-white Westie, who had burrowed under the snow, was lost for over two hours. One of my daughters suffered frostbite on her hands while trying to dig out and rescue the pooch. Fluffy began to dread being put outside to do her business.

December

Getting out of our driveway became an ordeal, since the snowplow operator was continually creating massive six-foot snow mountains, usually right after I had just shoveled my way out.

The snowplow driver had ripped away the PEACE ON EARTH, GOOD WILL TO MEN sign from my neighbors' nativity scene, and it stood atop the gigantic snow monument he had left in my driveway, as if mocking me. I swear that I'll wrap that peace sign around the guy's neck—after I've punched him in the nose—if I ever track him down!

I shambled through the snow over to my neighbor's house to return their peace sign, but I found out that they had left for a long vacation in Florida. Merry Christmas.

I told Agnes that if we were going to continue to live in this white hell we needed to trade in our car for a Zamboni.

We leave for Atlanta tomorrow.

*"CHIEF SAYS WINTER LOOKS BAD. THE OWL IS
GONE FROM THE MEADOW; THE WOLF IS IN
HIS DEN; THE CRICKET HAS LOST ITS TONGUE;
AND THERE'S A QUASI-STATIONARY LOW AT
500 MILLIBARS! "*

DICK'S MEMORIES

Robin's Mail

Robin once got this message from a viewer: "Dick Goddard is twice the man you will ever be!" (I was hoping for more.)

What a Turkey

Robin Swoboda Wagner invited me to a Thanksgiving dinner a few years ago. When the assemblage inquired why she wasn't eating the turkey, she warned that it probably wasn't cooked enough. Can't be too careful.

"Big Chuck" Schodowski and "Lil' John" Rinaldi helped out with the annual Woollybear Festival. Here they are emceeing the Woollybear 500 race in the 1980s. And I enjoyed appearing in skits on their show. I thought I looked great as Elvis in this Vegas number. (I'm not sure what Tim Taylor is dressed as.)

WOOLLYBEAR CATERPILLAR

by Dick Goddard

BY LATE SUMMER ADULT TIGER MOTHS (ISIA ISABELLA) GIVE BIRTH TO HUNDREDS OF TINY WOOLLYBEAR LARVA (CATERPILLARS) THE SIZE OF PENCIL DOTS!

WOOLLYBEAR LARVA ARE 1/2 to 2 INCHES LONG WITH DARK BROWN ENDS AND A RUST-COLORED MIDDLE. THEY SPEND ALL WINTER AS A CATERPILLAR, SINCE SUGAR-ALCOHOL IN THEIR BODIES KEEPS THEM FROM FREEZING.

LEGEND SAYS A WIDE RUSTY BAND FORETELLS LITTLE WINTER SNOW... A NARROW STRIPE FORECASTS HEAVY SNOW. FAT, FUZZY WOOLLIES PRESAGE A COLD WINTER... THIN COATS MEAN A MILD WINTER.

IN SPRING, AFTER MUNCHING ON DANDELION, CLOVER AND PLANTAIN WEED, THE CATERPILLAR SPINS A COCOON OUT OF ITS OWN HAIR.

ISABELLA TIGER MOTH'S WINGS ARE LIGHT ORANGE-YELLOW WITH TINY BROWN-PURPLE SPOTS.

AFTER A FEW WEEKS A TIGER MOTH EMERGES FROM ITS HAIRY HOME AND FLITS AWAY IN THE SUMMER SUN.

AS WOOLLYBEAR CATERPILLARS AGE, THEIR BROWN AND RUSTY COLORS LIGHTEN.

VERMILION OR BUST

THE 13 SEGMENTS OF A WOOLLYBEAR (SUPPOSEDLY) REPRESENT THE 13 WEEKS OF WINTER. **A** RECENT STUDY DISCOVERED THAT WOOLLYBEARS THAT LIVE ON THE GREENLAND ICECAP CAN SURVIVE FOR OVER 14 YEARS!

Lore and Lure of the Woollybear

"Every person who has ever been grand marshal has lost his job the following year— and the others have died."

—Tim Taylor, introducing Dick Goddard at the 1992 Cleveland Emmy Awards and explaining why he considered it a dubious honor to be grand marshal of the annual Woollybear Parade

"TELL US WHY, MR. JOHNSON, YOU FEEL WE ARE IN FOR A HARD WINTER."

American pioneers and colonists closely observed the weather and nature for very practical reasons. Living in an agrarian society, they were constantly at the mercy of crop-killing droughts and unseasonable freezes. (Diaries from 1816 lamented the bitterly cold "Year Without a Summer.")

Visible weather events and circumstances were keenly remembered, and if they were repeated often enough, the signs became rules. Thus began the art of folklore forecasting.

Those who were most affected by the weather, especially farmers and sailors, often put their meteorological observations into easily remembered sayings or proverbs, and these adages were then handed down from generation to generation. Although no weather proverb has been given the American Meteorological Society's Seal of Approval, that is not because they have no degree of accuracy. It is that the sayings are not true at all times in all places.

Weather lore, including sayings or adages, runs the gamut from common

sense to misconception to superstition to wishful thinking. There are no infallible weather signs, but those that have a reasonably high percentage of accuracy do have a scientific basis.

Sky color has long been recognized as a portent of weather change, and the most famous weather rhyme of them all is related to the color red. This familiar proverb, which appears in the Bible (in Matthew, Chapter 16) and relates to a shepherd, is now most often heard in the following nautical couplet:

> *Red sky at dawning, sailor take warning;*
> *Red sky at night, sailor's delight.*

Because the wavelength of the color red is best able to penetrate a very dry and dusty atmosphere, that color has long been associated with fair weather. A red horizon in the evening tells you that a layer of dry, dusty air is to the west. Considering the general west-to-east movement of weather at this latitude, this suggests that the air currently to the west will be overhead the next day, bringing fair skies. The other portion of the forecast is not as accurate, however, as the red sky at sunrise implies that the dry air has already passed by, which may not be so.

Every man is a damned fool at least five minutes every day; wisdom consists in not exceeding the limit.

—ELBERT HUBBARD

The color gray indicates there is a considerable quantity of water droplets suspended in the air, and there's a good chance that the tiny droplets will eventually grow large enough for gravity to pull them down:

Evening red and morning gray
help the traveler on his way;
Evening gray and morning red
Bring down a rain upon his head.

There's an interesting rhyme that dates from pioneer days regarding the color of lightning in a thunderstorm:

Yaller gal, yaller gal, flashing through the night,
Thunderstorms will pass you by, unless the color's white.

There is some validity to the observation that yellowish lightning will never reach you, but white lightning will. The more distant the lightning, the better the chance that particles in the air will give the flash a yellow tint.

To the folklore forecaster, a golden amber sky at sunset foretells a windy day but no rain. A pale yellow sky at sunset warns of rain the next day.

On rare occasions the color green can be seen at the start of a sunrise or sunset. It is a brilliant and beautiful green ray that lasts for only an instant, and it's considered a good luck omen in many cultures. To the Scottish Highlander, just one fleeting glimpse of the green ray guarantees that you will never be deceived in love.

Winter-weather folklore forecasts are the most numerous and the most enduring. Even today these autumnal signs have their advocates and involve such disparate things as the thickness of the hair on animals and the abundance of acorns. In reality, a thick coat on a critter is most likely telling you that the animal is in good health, while a proliferation of acorns in September testifies to adequate rainfall during the growing season.

It is here that I must plead guilty—and I request charitable treatment by the Ameri-

Just a few of the decals I've created for the Woollybear Festival over the years.

"Lil' John" Rinaldi shared the microphone with me at the 1975 Woollybear Festival. Behind him are my daughter, Kim, and Woollybear co-founder "Mo" Coe.

can Meteorological Society. Since my early days on television I have, tongue-in-cheek, publicized the woollybear caterpillar as a winter-weather forecast prophet.

The woollybear is a dark-brown caterpillar with a lighter, rust-colored band around the middle. Legend says that if the dark ends crowd the rusty ring into a narrow band, a snowy winter lies ahead. If the rusty ring is wide and the dark-brown bands at each end are small, a snow-free winter is coming up.

Woollybears that are fat and fuzzy in autumn supposedly warn of a very cold winter, while the more hairless larvae presage a mild winter. The woollybear caterpillar has thirteen segments, and folklorists who are true believers go so far as to say that they represent each week of the winter season.

The woollybear caught on. Driving home one year from the Valley City Frog Jump in Medina County, I asked my daughter, Kim, what she thought of a similarly wacky festival devoted to the legendary weather-forecasting caterpillar, the woollybear. It sounded just goofy enough, so, with her seal of approval, the project was born.

I asked my TV8 colleague Neil Zurcher to see if there was any interest out there in starting a charity event to rival Valley City's. In scouting for a festival site, I told him, he'd probably have to find some nice folks who were just a little "off center," and who had a great sense of humor. That was in 1972.

A number of months later, Neil came by and announced that his talent search was over. The sponsor would be the Florence Elementary School Parent-Teacher Organization, and the people willing to stake their reputations on a TV weatherman and a fuzzy worm would be Maureen (Mo) Coe, Pat Zaleski, Donna Angelo, and Dottie Kudela.

The first Woollybear Festival was held on a sunny and warm Sunday in late October 1973 in the little town of Birmingham, six miles south of Vermilion in southeastern Erie County. Several hundred folks showed up. The miniparade consisted of the Firelands Falcons High School Marching Band, a few kids dressed up as caterpillars, and several Boy Scout troops. We seriously considered the possibility of having the parade units go around a second time. The winner of the caterpillar race was a highly suspect larva

Getting the word on winter from a scarf-wearing woollybear in the early days of the festival.

Kids in woollybear costumes are an important part of the Woollybear Festival, and a whole group joined us at the anchor desk in the festival's early days in the early 1970s. Behind the desk, from left, are sportscaster Jim Mueller, news anchor Jim Hale, me, and news anchor Jeff Maynor.

named Tommy, probably a salt marsh caterpillar. After the last woollybear caterpillar had raced, the consensus was that we had all had a very nice time. Not only that, but the local volunteer fire department and some other organizations had made a few bucks selling cider, doughnuts, pumpkins, and toy caterpillars.

So, we decided to do it again . . . and again . . . and again.

By the eighth festival in tiny Birmingham, the crowds had grown to more than 15,000. Parking was a major problem, and lawns were being trampled. When the local church appealed to us because the Sunday event was disrupting their activities, it was obvious that a new location had to be found.

In early 1980 we announced the need for a new and larger site. Thirteen towns and cities within the TV8 viewing area soon responded with calls and letters asking us to consider their venues. Of all the offers, it was the one from Vermilion that stood out as the most attractive.

The crowds had grown to more than 15,000.

Every promise made about Vermilion's ability to sponsor the Woollybear Festival has been fulfilled. You can't hold a city hostage for a whole day without irritating some of the townsfolk, but over the years the people of Vermilion have willingly given of their time and talents. As a result, the Woollybear has grown into one of Ohio's—and the nation's—largest single-day events. (Have

Over the years my friends at Fox 8 have helped organize and host the Woollybear Festival. Here John Rinaldi shows that everyone is encouraged to wear a woollybear costume.

The average dog is a nicer person than the average person.

—ANDY ROONEY

you ever seen a larger worm festival?) From an estimated initial attendance of about 30,000 in 1981, crowd estimates over the years have approached 100,000.

And what memories we have stockpiled! One of my most cherished is of our first "fearless folklore forecaster," the late Leon (Bad News) Bates. Leon was a shy, likable fellow who truly communed with nature. Wearing his bib overalls, buffalo-plaid shirt, and an engineer's cap, he was the perfect picture of a rustic—a person who shunned the everyday world and who preferred to socialize with the creatures of the forest. He added authenticity and credibility to the job of folklore forecaster. The fact that Leon often declined a fresh shave for the festival simply added to his charm.

For years Leon was content just being Leon. Then, one incredible Woollybear Sunday, Leon arrived at the festival freshly shaven and heavily cologned, wearing a brand-new fedora and a spiffy leisure suit. Leon had succumbed to the siren call of celebrity . . . and we loved him all the more for it.

Willis "Good News" Gebhardt, a much-loved centenarian, succeeded Leon as the Woollybear Festival's fearless forecaster, and the job has now passed on to Bill "Sunny Skies" Summers.

It was shortly after the annual Fox 8 Woollybear Festival in Vermilion when I received a call from a doctor at the children's unit at Marymount South Hospital. The doctor asked if I had ever heard of someone eating a woollybear caterpillar.

DICK'S MEMORIES

Doney's Dilemma

Jim Doney was the host of Channel 8's popular *Adventure Road* for many years. He was occasionally assigned to do the weekend weather. I'll never forget the night he spent almost all of the weather program trying to locate the state of Wyoming. He never did.

I recalled a schoolmate of mine once chomping down on a firefly, but never a caterpillar. (Over the years I had jokingly suggested that in preparing woollybear dishes you should only use the tasty orange middle section, since the black ends are bitter—I will no longer do that!)

"Well," the doctor continued, "I have a seventeen-month-old who ate a woollybear."

My shock quickly subsided when the doctor said, "She's doing okay, but she did have an initial violent reaction."

Here's the incredible story: Little Jennifer Quayle and her parents, Lynn and Ken, were visiting Jennifer's grandmother, Florence Roseman, in Broadview Heights. The Quayles live on the Isle of Man, smack dab between England and Ireland.

"She's at the age when everything goes into her mouth," her dad told me, "and I blame what happened on her mum."

It seems that Jennifer's mother always gave her daughter raisins for treats, and when Jennifer was playing on the sun porch she saw this thing creeping along, and it looked like her favorite snack. Immediately after swallowing a good portion of the caterpillar, Jennifer started screaming and shouting. The little girl was having an adult-sized reaction to her mobile "raisin" treat.

Jennifer's face began to swell, and she broke out in an angry rash. Dad sped her to Marymount Hospital, and en route it appeared that the tot was passing out.

At the hospital's emergency room they tried to remove the caterpillar barbs stuck in Jennifer's mouth and lips. Unfortunately, the hairs were embedded in her skin. The medication that was promptly given to Jennifer quickly began to work, and it wasn't long before the barbs dissolved and fell out.

The doctor confided that in twenty-four years of helping patients he had "never seen anything like that before."

Jennifer made a fast recovery from

Dogs love their friends and bite their enemies, quite unlike people, who are incapable of pure love and always have to mix love and hate.

—SIGMUND FREUD

It's the Woollybear 500—the slow-speed race that's an annual feature of the Woollybear Festival.

her ordeal, and her grateful parents made an uneventful return trip to the Isle of Man (population 75,000, with no reported woollybears).

I called Florence Roseman several times to check on her grandchild's recovery and current health. Everything has come out well.

After a decent interval, I sent Grandma Florence a stuffed toy woollybear to give to Jennifer. I even offered to make Jennifer our Woollybear Queen and parade marshal when she next visits Northeast Ohio.

DICK'S MEMORIES

Bowled Over

I hosted *Bowling for Dollars* on TV8 in the '70s because of Bill Flynn, our hard-drinking general manager whom everybody loved. A lot of people auditioned for the job, but he picked me. Bill said, "You're the guy."

The philosophy of *Bowling for Dollars* was to build our audience with regular Clevelanders, and the station used it to their advantage. People would send in postcards to become a contestant, and the promotion department was told, "If anybody's name ends in a vowel, get 'em on the show."

We ran the show out of the station—they built an alley in the basement. The equipment came from Japan and had Japanese characters all over it. A good bowler had no advantage over a bad bowler because the alley was so lopsided. You could see the waves in the lane.

The basement set was OK in winter—almost, but not really. In the summer it was a sauna. The air conditioning made so much noise they had to turn it off when we were down there.

People would come up and be so nervous that when they were asked to introduce their friends in the audience, the camera would pan over and they'd forget the names. They'd loudly whisper, "What's your name?" and we'd all be perspiring.

It was bowling hell.

There is no psychiatrist on earth like a puppy licking your face.

—BEN WILLIAMS

DICK'S PALS

Illusion Destroyed

JOE BENNY: We were planning the show on a Friday during the savings and loan crisis in the 1980s. We were going to work on a bunch of stories for the six o'clock segment, and I called local universities to see if anybody could come on and talk about the impact for the average person.

Somebody from Case or Cleveland State said they could come out to the station, and I said we'd probably put him on in the second half hour to talk with Tim and Robin. He said, "Great! I love your station. I've watched Dick Goddard for years. I'd love to meet everybody."

I told him we'd do that—just come around 6:30, tell security who you are, I'll come and get you, and we'll do some TV. He said, "Great!"

Every Friday for as long as I can remember, Goddard gave away dogs and cats. We'd have a field day watching some of the people who brought in fleabags for people to adopt, and Dick would be walking down the hall with them, talking and jotting notes—its name, whether the animal had been spayed or neutered, and so on.

At 6:30 I got the call in the control room: "Your guest is here." Right on time, it's going well. I went down and got the guy, and he was really nervous. "I can't wait to meet Dick and Tim and Robin," he said. Don't worry, I said, we'll make sure when you're done you get to meet everybody.

We went up the elevator and started down the long hall to the studio. Wow, I said, something really smells vile. Like an outhouse. It hadn't smelled that way when I went downstairs.

Right in the middle of the hallway, under the "On Air" sign you'd see opening the *Big Chuck & Lil' John* show, there's Goddard, bending over. The Friday adoption dog had crapped all over. In fact, its legs were apart, it was still going, and this toothless guy who brought it in is trying to pull it down the hall. The odor is starting to overpower the entire hallway. And there's Goddard trying to pick up the mess with paper, and here comes my professor.

Dick didn't blink an eye.

"Just a minute," he said. "I want to shake your hand, but the company just gave me a new raise, and I dropped it and I'm picking it up."

Another illusion destroyed.

I went into the studio and told Tim what the dog just did. He said, "Better there than here."

The professor said, "Wow—TV's really different than what I thought."

Money is a good servant but a bad master.

—FRANCIS BACON, SR.

If there are no dogs in Heaven, then when I die I want to go where they went.

—WILL ROGERS

FOX 8
Pet Parade

Thanks to the generosity of my television employers, I have been able to offer dogs and cats for adoption since May 1980. There have been so many stories. Once, a kitten got loose before one show and was lost in the station for two days. We found her in just about the last place we could have looked: the extensive videotape rack.

We've had every emetic experience possible. My favorite was the time that Robin Swoboda's cat (she was holding it on the anchor desk) presented her with not just vomit, but a nice selection of tapeworms. Great for the evening dinner-hour viewers.

My worst experience came the first week I was allowed to present the animals. A little Benji-type dog was too much for the nice couple in Parma who had called to adopt him. So I told them I'd drive over to pick up the dog and place her with another family. The dog had nipped the lady, but she was a nice soul and didn't make a big deal out of it.

I had just picked up a shiny new car that afternoon, a very warm and humid day in May. The air conditioning wasn't working, and that really upset me. I drove the car to Parma, picked up the pooch, and got into a massive traffic snarl on the way back to TV8. The little guy was restless, and I couldn't roll down the windows very far since I knew the rascal would try to jump out of the car. As a result, the small car became a greenhouse.

As the pooch was hopping back and forth from the front seat to the back, I suddenly perceived an abominable odor. Right. Little Benji had responded to nature's call . . . directly over the

Animal adoption volunteers from Lorain County joined me around the time we started "Pet Parade" in 1980. I'm sure we've had several thousand adoptions since then.

gearshift box, just to my right. It was stop-and-go in traffic for what would be the longest thirty-five minutes of my life. The aroma was overpowering. Perspiration was streaming down my face, and as people would pull up alongside me and wave, I tried my best to smile back, pretending I was having a nice day. My other problem, amid the major problem of doggie diarrhea, was that Benji kept jumping from the passenger seat into my lap, depositing a few souvenirs en route.

I finally arrived at the television station and almost tore the car door off trying to get out into the fresh air. I looked through the window and noticed that the pooch seemed to be smiling; at least he was wagging his soggy tail. Even so, I loved that little fella. It could happen to any of us.

To get your dog or cat on the Fox 8 Pet Parade, you can call any Monday at 7 p.m. The pet lady will answer the phone at 216-432-4222.

You make a fool of yourself with a dog, and not only will he not scold you, but he will make a fool of himself too.

—SAMUEL BUTLER

Whoever said you can't buy happiness forgot about puppies.

—ANONYMOUS

Celebrity visitors to TV8 included Benji the movie dog.

DICK'S PALS

The Great Camera Caper and Sequels

TIM TAYLOR: Dick is a genius, but people have no idea—he has no sense of social propriety, which is why he gets into trouble. In church he is always inappropriate.

Example: Tana Carli was my co-anchor from 1981 to 1983 and the first female co-anchor in the history of Cleveland television. The story of her wedding ceremony is known in the annals of TV8 as "The Great Camera Caper."

It was a high Mass, during which we knew picture snapping was simply not appropriate. The seriousness of the occasion apparently escaped Dick. Even the priest coming down and giving him an admonishing glare couldn't stop his pictorial frenzy. In fact, when he finally ran out of film, Dick was so eager to reload as quickly as possible that he wasn't even paying attention. Whether it was carelessness or just plain bad luck is inconsequential. He thought he had rewound the roll of film in the camera. But when he opened it, the celluloid sprang out and coiled like a snake around his fingers, making all kinds of noise. Our pew was rocking; I was crying with laughter, and Dick was feverishly working to stuff the spaghetti-like mess back into the camera. Finally he managed to slam the camera shut, with film sticking out around the edges. Adding to the comedy of this event, after the ceremony we noticed for the first time he was the only one in the sea of somber black, navy, and charcoal suits wearing a checked sport coat—which, incidentally, he wears to this day on the air. When asked about his choice, he said he didn't realize it was such a serious occasion.

Enter Denise D'Ascenzo, my co-anchor from 1983 to 1986, another beautiful and intelligent young woman, but much more serious than we were used to. In fact, during the relatively short time she spent with Goddard and me, Denise became known as the nothing-to-live-for queen. We eventually learned that much of her reserve stemmed from a long-distance relationship—her fiancé ran a family business in New England.

When the lovely Tana Carli married TV8 general manager Joe Dimino in 1983, I knew the one thing lacking in the bride's trousseau was a woollybear sticker. (Courtesy of Tana Carli)

What was perhaps the defining moment of her Cleveland career came at Goddard's annual Woollybear Festival parade. Denise, late as usual, ran toward an already-moving open convertible along the Vermilion parade route. She jogged toward the convertible we were to share just as the driver reached the reviewing stand. Just as she raised one of her extraordinarily long legs to jump over the closed door, the driver's wife tried to help her by suddenly flinging the door open, with disastrous results. As the door sent Denise flying, the cheering and clapping instantly turned to a subdued "Ohhhh," followed by a deadly silence as my embarrassed co-anchor lay sprawled on her back, attempting to maintain what was left of her dignity in the middle of Vermilion's main drag. Seeing that only her ego was injured, Dick tried to save the day by asking the crowd to clap long and hard if they wanted Denise to remain in Cleveland. No one was listening. Silence. That would be Denise's last Woollybear Festival. She's now happily married and living in New England.

Enter the irrepressible Robin Swoboda, about whom I could write a novel.

She had heard about the Great Camera Caper. At Robin's wedding to then-Browns punter Bryan Wagner in San Diego, she alerted everybody that there would be no cameras. Dick does not follow rules—he doesn't even hear them. After we were all seated and he's ready to start shooting, one of the ushers slips behind him and plucks the camera out of his hand. Robin looks behind her and starts laughing. She got him. The lightning raid happened so quickly that the usually nimble-witted Goddard was for the first time at a loss for words.

Dick is oblivious to protocol. We went to the wake of a great guy who had worked at the station for many years. Right ahead of us was the casket, and I immediately went over. Dick looked at me and said, "Where is he?" I said, "I believe he's the one in the casket."

> *The Jews and Arabs should sit down and settle their differences like good Christians.*
>
> —*WARREN ROBINSON AUSTIN*

> *When asked what he thought about western civilization, Mahatma Gandhi replied, "I think it would be a good idea."*

DICK'S MEMORIES

TV Terrorist

It was in the late '80s when a twelve-year-old took over control of the studio cameras at Channel 8. One of our film editors had brought his boy to work so he could watch the late-night news. The young man was somehow able to don a headset, with microphone attached, and he began to call the shots during the news program. I first became aware of the problem when Vince Cellini, our sports anchor, came into the newsroom laughing hysterically.

Starry, Starry Nights

If you think education is expensive, try ignorance.

—DEREK BOK

The Stump Hill Exotic Animal Farm in Massillon cares for wild animals that pet owners and even zoos have difficulty managing. The farm has more than 300 animals such as reindeer, grizzly bears, and large cats.

In our hurry to step off the daily treadmill of life in order to just sit and relax, it's easy for us to ignore the great celestial show that is there for us to see every night in the Northeast Ohio sky. True, from November into March clouds often keep the curtain closed on the performance, but when skies are clear—and you're far enough away from the glare and murky air of the cities— the stars and planets are dazzling. On an unusually clear night here we can see about two thousand twinkling stars with the unaided eye. The stars we see at night, of course, do not simply go away during the daytime; the light from our sun is so blindingly bright that we can't see them.

A star is a fiery atomic furnace, and these massive balls of glowing gas shine by their own light. Stars, like humans, are born, live out their lives, and die. The ordinary star we call our sun is considered to be middle-aged, suitably bulging out at the middle, with another five billion years to live before its atomic fuel runs out.

It's easy to confuse stars, which shine on their own, with planets such as Earth, which shine by reflecting sunlight. (If the sun blinked out, so would all the planets.) Planets are either rocky balls, like Earth, or giant balls of cold gas, like Jupiter. The thing we call our solar system is made up of the sun and all the objects that circle it: nine known planets, their moons, comets, asteroids, and meteors.

We see different stars during each season of the year, and that is because our planet is revolving as it orbits the sun. During winter, for example, we will see the same stars in the same place at the same time as the previous winter.

Although stars are moving away from us at unbelievable speed, their positions in the sky will not change during the short life span of a human. (The stars you see tonight were seen by Julius Caesar.) The light that reaches our eyes tonight from the supergiant star Rigel—which is five hundred light years away and twenty thousand times as bright as our mellow yellow sun—left that star before the birth of Columbus.

Stars are so incomprehensibly far away that astronomers calculate the distances in light years. A light year is the distance light travels (at 186,282 miles per second) in one year. In that time, traveling at the speed of light, you would cover nearly six trillion earth miles (one trillion is one thousand billion). The nearest star to Earth, aside from our sun, is Alpha Centauri, some 4.3 light years away. It would take Neil Zurcher in a One Tank Trip spaceship traveling at one million miles per hour about 2,882 earth years to reach Alpha Centauri (and the accommodations aren't that nice).

You can easily judge the character of a man by how he treats those who can do nothing for him.

—JOHANN WOLFGANG VON GOETHE

DICK'S MEMORIES

Warbling Weatherman

I do love to sing. I've sung with the Cleveland Pops over a dozen times, usually a patriotic thing. I do the anthem a lot, but I've never done it at an Indians or Browns game.

At Channel 3 we had *The Mike Douglas Show*, where I was able to sing occasionally. They knew I was in musicals at Kent State, and a lady called and said, "Get Goddard to sing on your show." So they did, and any time a guest didn't show up, they'd say, "Get Goddard in here." I was able to sing to Zsa Zsa Gabor on the show and a couple of other ladies, too.

We had the noon news just before the show. I was just a kid off the farm, chalking away at the weather board. One day I heard a voice behind me: "Do you have any idea what you're doing there?" It was Bob Hope! I met a lot of real celebrities. They had a young Barbra Streisand as co-host for a week—and management at the station erased what she did for editorials so they didn't waste the tape. All those treasures got zapped.

"WHOEVER TOLD YOU THAT YOU COULD SING?"

While the positions of distant stars are considered to be fixed in our sky, the relatively nearby planets continually move to new locations. (The word *planet* is from the Greek word meaning "wanderer.") To visualize this, imagine that you are riding a merry-go-round while eight of your friends are walking around the carousel. Each time you reach the same point in your ride the trees and buildings (stars) are exactly where they were before. Your friends (planets) have become scattered about the park (especially if they've had an argument).

Our five brother and sister planets that are visible with the naked eye are Venus, Mars, Jupiter, Saturn, and Mercury (faint, at best). At least one of the planets is visible every night; sometimes several are.

Although it seems as if the stars and planets are racing around the earth, that is an illusion. It is the earth that is turning—counterclockwise. If you face south and are willing to invest half an hour of your time, you will notice that the stars are moving slowly from left to right (east to west). Once they have made it into the west they appear to dive toward the horizon, from upper left to lower right.

As recently as 1920, our universe was thought to be a single formation of stars. Since then, giant telescopes have shown that the cosmos is filled with cities of suns called galaxies. (Every star you see in the Northeast Ohio sky without the aid of a telescope is in the Milky Way galaxy.) The Hubble Space Telescope, launched in April 1990, has revealed that there are at least 50 billion galaxies in the universe, and that each galaxy contains billions (perhaps trillions) of stars. Planet Earth is located at an obscure ZIP code on the edge of a spiraling arm of the Milky Way galaxy. We have no idea where the Milky Way is positioned in the firmament because there may be no center to the universe.

The Milky Way is itself a spiral galaxy that is 100,000 light years across, which means it would take a spaceship traveling at the speed of light 100,000 years to get from one end to the other—and a light year is nearly six trillion earth miles. And that's just our galaxy. Altogether, there may be 100 billion galaxies in the uni-

If something is in me which can be called religious then it is the unbounded admiration for the structure of the world so far as our science can reveal it.

—ALBERT EINSTEIN

"REMEMBER. IF WE'RE NOT SCARING THE HELL OUT OF OUR VIEWERS WE'RE NOT DOING OUR JOB!"

verse, each containing some 100 billion stars. We are truly a mote in God's eye.

A constellation is a grouping of stars that was given a name by ancient astronomers who believed that the star pattern resembled an animal, an object, or a mythical god or hero. Within constellations are smaller patterns that are called asterisms—the Big Dipper in the constellation Ursa Major (the Great Bear) is an example.

The most familiar cluster of them all, the Big Dipper, is the key to finding any star in the Northeast Ohio sky. For example, by drawing a line from the "pouring" side of the Dipper you are led to the North Star, Polaris. Polaris, which is also called the Pole Star, is important because it is almost always in the same place, and is almost exactly north (at our latitude the North Star appears about halfway up in the sky). All other stars revolve counterclockwise around the Pole Star once each day. While Polaris appears rather faint to us, that is only because it is four million billion miles away. Polaris is actually 1,600 times as bright as our sun, and the light we see left the star about 350 years ago.

Jack the dog is a stray who stayed. He's the newsroom mascot at Fox 8.

For those who would like to learn more about the fascinating field of astronomy, there are two excellent monthly publications available at most bookstores: *Sky & Telescope* and *Astronomy*.

Don't be misled by the annual Christmastime scam that claims to—for a fee—name and certify a star for whomever you request. Grandma may be a stellar person, but stars can only be named, and authenticated, by the International Astronomical Union.

DICK'S MEMORIES

Can't Handle the Truth

For years, NBC began its news programs in the evening with a rotating globe. The globe was circling clockwise, instead of counterclockwise. I contacted NBC and was told to "stick to the weather." The rotation was eventually corrected.

Dennis's Wedding

TIM TAYLOR: When Dennis Kucinich married Elizabeth Harper in August 2005, he invited people he knew from his early days at city hall. Dennis knew a lot of people, and we were invited. It was an outdoor wedding, on the mall outside City Hall. We were seated next to Sean Penn. Dick was on his right and Cathy, my wife, and I were on the left.

Now, who in the world doesn't know about Sean Penn and the number of photographers he's taken out over the years? But this was Dick, and we heard him asking Sean Penn if he minds if Dick takes his picture.

There's a picture of that moment. Look at the looks on the faces. My wife is breaking up. I look the other way. Carl Monday's head jerks around. Penn said very politely, "I'm a guest here, as you are. I would hope you would respect my anonymity here."

Dick was baffled. So he invited Sean Penn to the Woollybear Festival. Priceless.

After the ceremony, they took pictures and said there would be a one-hour delay, and then we would adjourn to the City Hall rotunda for the reception. To pass the time, we went from the mall to the hotel bar nearby. Dick, like a magnet working, was attracted to Shirley MacLaine, who brought her dog to the wedding. She was seated with Sean Penn and her escort. We wanted to give them their space, so we smiled and kept going—and watched. Dick started petting her dog. She said, "Please don't pet him; he's very leery of people and he's sleeping." Of course she had no idea who Goddard was.

Dick is like a little kid. He has no sense of propriety, which is why he gets into trouble. Instead of just backing off, he proceeded to tell her, "You know, Shirley, while you were in movies, I was starring in *Damn Yankees* at Kent State," and broke into a refrain of "You Gotta Have Heart." We were dying. She had no idea who Goddard was. He saw it was not going anywhere and sort of slithered off.

We were trying to maintain some decorum, but that was followed by Shirley's encounter with him when he decided to get his picture with her dog, which she had set down next to her. Dick got down and basically crawled up to pet the dog, looking up from under the table while his buddy is snapping the picture. Shirley looks down, sees him, and says, "Get the (bleep) off my dog!"

Dick was baffled. You could not make this stuff up.

This is a very candid scene from video shot at the wedding of Dennis Kucinich and Elizabeth Jane Harper in 2005. I'm seated next to Sean Penn, who is wearing a white shirt, and I had just asked him about coming to the Woollybear Festival. You can imagine the response. And you can see the reaction from my buddy Kenny Moehring, next to me, and Carl Monday, behind me, and especially from Cathy and Tim Taylor in the foreground. "You embarrass me," Tim said.

School Daze

Aside from nitrogen, the second most common element on Earth is stupidity. Artificial intelligence can be no match for natural brain atrophy.

The politically correct schoolteacher of today is shackled by society—and lawyers—when it comes to reprimanding or criticizing a student. I was in high school in the post–World War II 1940s. One of our teachers was an ex-marine, and on several occasions he felt obligated to put a recalcitrant student in a headlock. That really gave us encouragement to study.

I imagine that, although physically larger, the youth of this decade are neither more nor less intelligent than those of my decade. Computers and electronics have opened so many more doors for those who will take advantage of the opportunities.

Many athletes today not only excel in their chosen sport, but are exemplars in the classroom as well. Some schools, however, are still more than willing to grant scholarships to those who don't qualify academically. Shelby Metcalf, the basketball coach at Texas A&M University, tried to light a fire under a star Aggie freshman who told the coach he was ineligible because he had just pulled down four Fs and one D. "Son," said Metcalf, "it looks like you've been spending too much time on one subject."

Whether it is because so many students in this country's school systems have no desire to learn or are being inadequately taught, educational level tests reveal an alarming lack of knowledge in nearly all subjects, especially science, mathematics, and geography. The tests show that about one-third of all students, including college freshmen, cannot properly point out their correct state, county, and home town on a map.

We give dogs time we can spare, space we can spare, and love we can spare. And in return, dogs give us their all. It's the best deal man has ever made.

—M. FACKLAM

A dog is the only thing on earth that loves you more than he loves himself.

—JOSH BILLINGS

DICK'S MEMORIES

Kinnan's Classic

Wally Kinnan, my forecasting friend from Channel 3, didn't tolerate weather fools gladly. Greyhound Bus Lines was a sponsor of his weathercasts and, responding to a critic of his efforts, he announced that he'd like to see that fellow "under the next Greyhound bus leaving town!"

A science question on Ben Franklin's experiment with lightning (he flew a kite into a thunderstorm in 1752) was answered thusly: "Ben Franklin invented electricity by rubbing two cats together, backwards."

Euclid no doubt began spinning in his grave (counterclockwise, of course) when a student made this geometric revelation: "Lines with three sides that have angles of 135 degrees are called obscene triangles."

Problems in the gigantic New York City school system can only be imagined. Frazzled teachers are required to make comments on all students' report cards. Following are some of the most eloquent. (Supervisors who issued reprimands no doubt had to smile and pay homage to David Letterman.)

Nature never deceives us; it is always we who deceive ourselves.

—*JEAN JACQUES ROUSSEAU*

"I BELIEVE HE WANTS TO GO OUT."

Since my last report, your child has reached rock bottom and has started to dig.

I would not allow this student to breed.

Your child has delusions of adequacy.

Your son is depriving a village somewhere of an idiot.

Your son sets low personal standards and then consistently fails to achieve them.

This child has been working with glue too much.

When your daughter's IQ reaches 50, she should sell.

The gates are down, the lights are flashing, but the train isn't coming.

If this student were any more stupid, he'd have to be watered twice a week.

It's impossible to believe the sperm that created this child beat out 1,000,000 others.

DICK'S PALS

The Animals Come First

JOE BENNY: The animals always came first with Dick. I was doing the six [o'clock news] one evening, a nice summer day, and started paging him to go on: "Goddard to the studio, Goddard to the studio." He didn't show up or answer the page, and I didn't know where the hell he was. "Goddard to the studio. Goddard, where the hell are you?" I started stretching and moving segments, pushing up John O'Day's Money Minute. Where the hell was Goddard? I went to the newsroom and saw Mark Koontz. "I have not seen him," he said. "He left—he ran out of here a while ago."

Finally Dick comes back into the building. I asked where the hell he was.

"Well, I saw a spider in the newsroom, so I grabbed it and walked it out to the back field behind the station and let it go."

In the studio three weeks later, Loree Vick said, "There's a spider!" and pointed to the floor. I stepped on it and said to Dick, "You'll be on time tonight."

Don't Panic

ED BYERS: Dick was our weather guy on the old WGAR, the Big 1220, when John O'Day and I anchored the news on John Lanigan's morning show. He did the "WGAR Clima-cast," and I loved the way he'd say it. He would get up at 4:30 a.m. to start putting his forecast together for radio. This guy just went to bed, after getting home from the 11 o'clock news on TV, and he's getting up to do it again. And if there was severe weather approaching, he would stay with us until we went off the air at 10.

We all have phobias. When I was a kid in Niles, mine was thunderstorms. I'd watch Dick every night. He has a way of explaining weather to people, to not get them riled up. A lot of forecasting now is scare tactics—"It's snowmageddon!" or whatever—but with Dick you know the sun will come up again tomorrow. I've talked to more people who have weather phobias, and they're Goddard people because he explains it like a doctor with a good bedside manner. He has a calming way about him.

Ed Byers, media manager for Medical Mutual of Ohio, was known as Ed Richards during his years as a newsman on WGAR radio.

Skipper, the Lake County Captains' mascot, looks a bit like a large, green woollybear.

Weather Wisdom According To Kids

If you think dogs can't count, try putting three dog biscuits in your pocket and then give him only two of them.

Weather is taught in most elementary schools today. In fact, a steady flow of mail from budding meteorologists lands on my desk during the school year. The children usually ask weather questions or request weather maps and pictures. Over the years I have accumulated a priceless treasure of letters from small fry, especially second and third graders.

Quite often the letter is addressed to Mr. Garter, Mr. Gutter, or Mr. Gotter. Within the letter there sometimes emerges a pearl of truth and honesty that could only come from the uncomplicated mind of a child. Whenever the isobars misbehave or six inches of partly sunny falls, I can brighten my day by thumbing through the file marked "letters from kids." Here are a few gems:

Our class is studying the wether, please send us maps and things. P.S. I do not watch you. My parents watch Channel 3.

When the news begins I always like to watch until you come on.

The hole 27 kids in my class are writting a letter. I am in the second grade so if you find any mestakes it is not my fault.

Please send informashun on weather. Please hurray. P.S. I got a big sister 36-40-38.

We apresheate you coming to our school. We were lucky. We got off gym.

"THIS SUGGESTION COMES FROM W.K. IN NORTH RIDGEVILLE."

We have to watch you every night.
Even when there is a good program on.

I would like a whether chart about tornados and
hurricans. I watch your show at 6 and 11. I am a teecher
and we are studdying the clouds. Your frinde, Mrs. Larko.

Some children have offered little-known weather facts and observations:

A January fog will freeze a hog.

If you look at the full moon over your left shoulder you will die.

Wind is air that gets pushy.

A gentleman from France is called a monsoon.

Teachers always tell their students that they can determine how far away from them a thunderstorm is by counting the number of seconds between seeing the lightning flash and hearing the thunder (add one mile for every five seconds of delay . . . a fifteen-second delay, for example, tells you that a thunderstorm is centered three miles from you). A teacher sent me this student's explanation of the phenomenon:

You can listen to thunder after lightning and tell how close you come to
getting hit. If you don't hear it then you got hit, so never mind.

Here are a few more statements and opinions that teachers have shared with me:

There is one good way to tell between a high and a low pressure. One of
them makes it rain but I can't think which one it is.

It is so hot in some parts of the world that the people who live there have
to live some where else.

My goal in life is to be as good a person as my dog thinks I am.

The beginning of wisdom is when you realize how little you know. The wisest profess they know nothing.

—SOCRATES

At my desk at TV8, I'm looking over a facsimile map and checking some details by phone.

The fancy KYW-TV set in 1962.

BELIEVING GODDARD

Junk Science

The American public has a large appetite for disasters, and the business of writing books based on junk science has been highly profitable. Doomsday publications on such topics as the next ice age, the greenhouse effect, and coming celestial calamities are continually cranked out, in hope that the gullible public will buy enough to warrant a script for a follow-up movie or a television special.

I'm surrounded! But I didn't mind at all, promoting the first Woollybear Festival in Birmingham in 1973.

One of the most egregious examples of this came in the late 1970s when a book called *The Jupiter Effect* began to ring up sales. The idea was that a straight lineup (conjunction) of several planets in our solar system—featuring the giant gas ball Jupiter—would cause gravity to tug on the earth's surface with such force that it would trigger massive earthquakes, seaquakes, and tsunamis. In 1982, several months before the date of the planetary conjunction, the authors called a press conference to repent and say, in essence, "By Jove, there won't be a Jupiter Effect. We miscalculated." No money was refunded.

Even the media can be victimized by a scientific hoax. A few years ago a major wire service in this country distributed a story from a "respected British scientif-

It's soothsayers versus truthsayers. The skeptic's job is to slay a beautiful hypothesis on the lance of an ugly fact.

The exact contrary of what is generally believed is often the truth.

—*JEAN DE LA BRUYERE*

ic organization" that had determined that the reason there were so many tornadoes in the United States was that Americans drove on the right side of the highways. It was the swift passing of automobiles on warm days that created a massive counterclockwise vortex of wind. The British study also revealed that most of the tornadoes occurred in rural areas on weekends when city dwellers were making a mad dash for the countryside.

As the authorities on education in this country tell us, science illiteracy and mathematical innumeracy are the norm. While worry over the pollution of our environment is unquestionably a legitimate concern, we must be on the alert for alarmists. Consider the concern over the proliferation of the chemical "dihydrogen monoxide." A petition to ban further use of this substance was signed by forty-three of the fifty people who were approached with the following list of dihydrogen monoxide's effects:

- It is found in tumors of fatally ill cancer patients.
- In its gaseous state it can cause severe burns.
- Excessive inhalation can kill.
- It can cause baseball-sized objects to critically impact on the unwary.
- It is a major component of acid rain.
- It can devastate entire communities.

What is dihydrogen monoxide? Water.

DICK'S MEMORIES

Whoops

Management at Fox 8 has allowed me to present dogs and cats for adoption for more than thirty years. I try to remember the names of both the people and the pets who have been on the shows. As I'm standing in a line at a check-out counter, a lady turned to me and said that was she was sorry to tell me that Otto had died.

"How sad," I said. "Wasn't he a schnauzer?"

"No," she said. "He was my husband."

Letter from a viewer, 1977

Your wooly bear festival is a classic example of the violation of God's word in Ex 20:1–7. Humanity continues to ignore these commandments with its idolatry, statue renovations, dog face masks, Halloween costumes, the false worship of Christmas which is not in the bible to be observed and thus is a doctrine of men, worship in vain, matt 15:7–9. Continue in these infractions of God's laws and this nation suffers. Already we have sick leadership, Mal 4:4–6, Isa 58:1.

Promoting *American Idol* brought Paula Abdul to Fox 8, and fate brought us together.

The Job of Being God

With the world population now around seven billion and growing every day, the percentage of ne'er-do-wells and sinners must be rising exponentially. This makes the job of being God tougher and tougher.

The wisdom of children can never be underestimated, and when third graders were asked to explain the job of being God, the results were heavenly:

> *One of God's main jobs is making people. He makes them to replace the ones that die so there will be enough people to take care of things on earth.*
>
> *He doesn't make grown-ups, just babies. I think that's because they are smaller and easier to make. That way he doesn't have to take up his valuable time teaching them to walk and talk. He can just leave that to mothers and fathers.*
>
> *God's second most important job is listening to prayers. An awful lot of this goes on, since some people, like preachers and things, pray at times beside bedtime.*
>
> *God doesn't have time to listen to the radio or TV because of this.*
>
> *Because he hears everything there must be a terrible lot of noise in his ears, unless he has thought of a way to turn it off.*
>
> *God sees everything and hears everything and is everywhere, which keeps him pretty busy. So you shouldn't go wasting his time by going over your mom and dad's head asking for something they said you couldn't have.*

I met pets of all varieties, and their often-lovely owners, at the Akron Pet Expo in 2009.

"I'M PUTTING YOU IN CHARGE OF THAT ONE."

Forgive, O Lord, my
little jokes on Thee,
and I'll forgive Thy
great big one on me.

—ROBERT FROST

Atheists are people who don't believe in God. I don't think there are any in Chula Vista. At least there aren't any who come to our church.

Jesus is God's son. He used to do all the hard work like walking on water and performing miracles and trying to teach the people who didn't want to learn about God. They finally got tired of him preaching to them and they crucified him.

But he was good and kind like his father and he told his father they didn't know what they were doing and to forgive them and God said, "OK."

His dad (God) appreciated everything that he had done and all his hard work on earth so he told him he didn't have to go out on the road anymore. He could stay in heaven. So he did. And now he helps his dad out by listening to prayers and seeing which things are important for God to take care of and which ones he can take care of himself without having to bother God. Like a secretary, only more important.

You can pray anytime you want and they are sure to hear you because they got it worked out so one of them is on duty all the time.

You should always go to church on Sunday because it makes God happy, and if there's anybody you want to make happy it's God.

Don't skip church to do something you think will be more fun like going to the beach. This is wrong! And, besides, the sun doesn't come out at the beach until noon anyway.

If you don't believe in God, besides being an atheist, you will be very lonely, because your parents can't go everywhere with you, like to camp, but God can.

It's good to know that he's around you when you're scared in the dark or when you can't swim very good and you get thrown into real deep water by the big kids.

But you shouldn't just always think of what God can do for you. I figure God put me here and he can take me back anytime he pleases.

And that's why I believe in God.

I'm no Einstein.

—ALBERT EINSTEIN

It is important to be quiet in church because people are sleeping

—A FIRST GRADER

If I have any beliefs about immortality it is that certain dogs I have known will go to heaven, and very, very few persons.

— JAMES THURBER

A man content to go to heaven alone will never go to heaven.

— BOETHIUS

You must believe in God in spite of what the clergy say.

—BENJAMIN JOWETT

He's as big as Big Bird, but he's Wolford the Woollybear, official mascot of the Woollybear Festival.

DICK'S MEMORIES

Unsportsmanlike Conduct

I'm a great sports fan, and I've had the pleasure of doing broadcast stats for the Cleveland Browns for more than forty years. The rivalry with the Pittsburgh Steelers is legendary. Don't even think about wearing seal brown and orange to a game in the Steel City. The ugliest scene I've ever witnessed came in the 1980s at old Municipal Stadium in Cleveland. The men's urinals were like pig troughs. As I headed for the broadcast booth I saw medics carrying a poor soul in a Steelers jacket out the door. He had become intoxicated (hard to believe), and some Browns fans kindly tried to sober him up by tossing him into the urinal, where he had been marinating for some time. Now that's ugly.

In the Name of Religion

With or without religion, good people will do good and evil people will do evil. But for good people to do evil, that takes religion.

—Physicist Steven Weinberg

Only two things are infinite, the Universe and human stupidity, but I'm not so sure about the Universe.

—Albert Einstein

A man content to go to heaven alone will never go to heaven.

—BOETHIUS

It has been said that nothing is so firmly believed as what we least know. So it is with religions. A survey by Pew Research showed that those who know the most about the most prominent faiths are the agnostics and atheists. Other names for the "nonbelievers" are Freethinkers and Truthseekers. These people claim that all religions are manmade, and that they originated before most people could read or write. Even God is a human invention, they say, and belief in a higher power came many thousands of years ago when our forebears sought an answer for the violence—earthquakes, volcanic eruptions, storms, and lightning, for example—that terrified them.

Scientists estimate that the universe formed about 15 billion years ago. They also believe that some 4.6 billion years ago a cloud of dust condensed into planet Earth and formed a layered globe, much like the windings in a golf ball, some 8,000 miles in diameter. Earliest humans appeared about 2 million years ago, and modern humans made their debut about 30,000 years ago. If human history were a twenty-four-hour day, humans wouldn't have appeared until the last two seconds. It is estimated that there are nearly 7 billion humans on planet Earth today, which is a fraction of all the humans who have ever lived. Technically, we are living in the Cenozoic Era. At least that is the scientific view of how everything has evolved.

According to Charlton Heston and fundamentalist religionists, there was a supreme being who created everything in just six days, some 6,000 years ago.

My wonderful parents and grandparents were kind and gentle people who imbued in me a love and respect for animals. My father's honesty was exemplary. Mom told me of the time my dad, who was an automobile mechanic, and a damned good one, returned a wallet to the driver who had lost it in his vehicle. This was during the Great Depression in the 1930s, when losing a wallet was a family catastrophe.

I'm telling you this because what follows will no doubt upset many of you. But, emulating my dad, I'm just being honest.

My parents were not overly religious, but while growing up in what is now the city of Green, south of Akron, I attended the United Methodist church and sang in the choir. The preacher was not a Bible-thumping, fire-and-brimstone type, and his sermons were believable. It wasn't until I was out of the military and attending Kent State University that I began to question the story of a talking snake and other phantasmagoria. Science and nature soon overtook religious scripture.

In my home library I have over one thousand books. With few exceptions they deal with philosophy, nature, history, science, religion, and mythology.

A man's worst enemies can't wish on him what he can think up for himself.

—FOLK SAYING

It was completely on the up-and-up, but of course there were questions afterward when my daughter, Kim, won the Woolly-bear Race at the festival in 1975. That's "Lil' John" Rinaldi with us.

DICK'S PALS

A Little Bit of Chaos

ROBIN SWOBODA: At my wedding, in San Diego, Dick was in the hotel lobby inviting people. To my wedding! He invited my mother! She said, "Yes, Dick, I know—I'm her mother." And Dick is infamous for taking pictures inappropriately and wreaking havoc and chaos. He revels in it. And it isn't just at events.

We had a tomato-growing contest one year. I talked about my tomatoes on the air, and Dick surprised me by getting a picture of them in my yard. I said, "How did you . . . Oh." Because then it all came together.

My neighbor Michele had called me in concern because she saw him in the yard but couldn't tell it was him. It was raining, so all she saw was a man in a trench coat, carrying an umbrella, hunkered over in my backyard.

If you can keep your head while those about you are losing theirs, you don't know what the hell is going on.

Guardian of Animal Life

"BIG CHUCK" SCHODOWSKI: Dick really is Mr. Nice Guy. He's the kind of guy who gets out of the shower to take a pee. And he really is a freak about animals. He's not only the protector of stray cats and dogs, he's the guardian of all animal life at TV8. Once during the news, they once started paging him—"Dick Goddard, get to the studio right away, Dick Goddard, twenty seconds." He went flying by, in the other direction, holding his arms out in front of him. He had a spider's web, with the spider in it, and he was taking it to the back door to release it outside. He'd bring in birds and nurse them back to health.

The Friend of Animals

TIM TAYLOR: Dick will be out on the interstate, and if he sees a stray in trouble he'll park his car. Cars are going by, and God love him, he saves these dogs. One day he saw what he thought was a dead dog in the road. Then the next day he saw it again, and he thought it had moved. It wasn't in the same place. Dick was so guilt-ridden, thinking maybe the dog was alive when he first saw it, that he stopped the car, stopped traffic, and saw that the dog was indeed dead. So he wrapped it—a dead dog off the road—in carpeting that he keeps in his car for animals. He took it home and buried it off the highway. He just loves animals.

After eight decades, I have concluded that we are living in the only hell there is. To live briefly, suffer debilitating diseases, and inevitably lose those you love makes any mythological hell seem absurd.

Hell has a different meaning to many. The French philosopher Jean-Paul Sartre said that "Hell is other people." In reality, our worst enemies could not conjure up the pure hell we make for ourselves on earth.

It was the Christians—and five hundred years before them, the Zoroastrians—who upgraded the place of eternal pain and suffering they called hell. Those who didn't follow the rules were destined to spend eternity in the fiery furnace as punishment for their earthly misdeeds. At the other extreme was a place called heaven, where the pious would spend endless time honoring the deity that created them. (One of the joys of being in heaven, claimed a famous saint, was being able to look down on the poor tormented souls who were suffering and writhing in pain—even your mother, family members, and friends, if they deserved the punishment.)

Without beer or football, what better entertainment could there be?

Many religions realized that in order to keep their followers in line they had to establish a place of punishment. Enter hell. Men soon realized how profitable the threat of eternal torment could be, and this became a celestial ATM.

When and how did hell originate? Hell came to us from the mythical Norse ice goddess, Hel. Interestingly, and understandably, for them hell was not a place of fire, but of intense cold. It was a dark and mysterious place, but not the massive, fiery torture chamber that Christians made of it. The Persians (present Iran) worshipped the sun god Ahura Mazda, but their high prophet, Zoroaster, did not believe that the misery of their flaming hell would go on forever. (It was from the celebration of the festival of Ahura Mazda, by the way, that the Christians usurped the date of their nativity, December 25th.)

With all the suffering and cruelty inflicted on humankind by a supposedly kind and benevolent supreme being, it became necessary to explain the reason for this anomaly. Enter the devil. To paraphrase Pogo Possum, "We have met the devil and he is us."

In 1997 several of Fox 8's on-air personalities received their own baseball card to coincide with the 1997 All Star Game.

I confess that I am an interdenominational skeptic. I also believe that Humpty Dumpty was pushed. Since there are over two thousand religions on this small planet, surely one of them must be right.

A recent estimate of the makeup of major religions on Earth counts 1 billion Christians, 1 billion Muslims, 800 million Hindi and 14 million Jews. Everyone is an infidel to the other guy's religion. As one skeptic has put it, "All religions mock and ridicule other religions. All are right."

No one—no matter how high they have risen in their religious hierarchy—can have any verifiable proof of why we are here or how we arrived. We are biological organisms living in a natural environment, nothing supernatural.

Many believe that there is a supernatural being who cares about each of us. That is a thought that gives enormous comfort and solace, even though it is a mystery as to why that supernatural being alternately rewards and punishes us.

The eminent British theoretical physicist Stephen Hawking has concluded that there is no need for a creator of the universe (He does not deny the possibility of such). That begs the obvious question: Who created the creator?

The search for the meaning of life cannot honestly be answered, although religions claim divine insight. Of thirty wars that have been fought over the last few decades, twenty-eight have been waged because of religious intolerance. History has shown that more people have been slain during religious wars than all purely political conflicts.

WJKW-TV8 would like to thank its viewers for making Newscenter 8 at noon, six and eleven the number one source of television news in Northeast Ohio.*

Thanks for coming home to Newscenter 8.

*Source: Feb. 1983, Cleveland ARB. Mon-Fri. Data subject to qualifications of the reports.

I know many Christians who are honest, loving, and caring. I know many agnostics and atheists who are also honest, loving. and caring. But I am unaware of any nonbeliever who has blown up an abortion clinic.

Most modern Christians are appalled by the behavior of the early church. Thousands of innocent souls were accused of being witches and warlocks during various inquisitions, and were subsequently burned at the stake—in-

DICK'S MEMORIES

Ice, He Said

I try to enunciate carefully on TV. My friend Mark Johnson at Channel 5 has a story why it's important. After one forecast where he warned, "You've gotta watch out for the black ice," he got a call from a guy who was all upset. "Whaddya mean by that?" the guy said. "The white guys aren't any better when it comes to drivin'!"

cluding one seven-year-old child at Wurzburg in 1629. The church acquired enormous wealth, since the property of the innocents was confiscated.

The behavior of some priests today reveals alarming abuse of their comforting ecclesiastical vows. The little girl who called was crying because her minister told her that she would never see her beloved pet in heaven because "animals have no souls." How blatantly cruel and unthinking. It is true that the Bible makes forty mentions of the dog—none favorably—and no mention of the cat, but there is absolutely no proof that any minister has such divine insight. As Will Rogers said, "If there are no dogs in heaven, I don't want to go there."

Even at this stage of man's evolution, many church leaders are scientifically illiterate. Some televangelists have most recently blamed volcanic eruptions, earthquakes, and tsunamis as punishment for man's sins. They should know that there is an earthquake on this small planet every ten minutes, and that volcanoes have been erupting from Earth's molten inner core ever since our planet was born. It's called nature.

Show me a televangelist who lives modestly—not in a mansion—who doesn't travel in a private jet with an entourage of sycophants, and who quotes from ALL verses of the Bible ("Don't become wealthy," Mark 10:21:25), and I'll show you an honest preacher.

I had the great good fortune to meet the late Carl Sagan, legendary astron-

A good education should leave a lot to be desired.

—ALAN GREGG

The truly educated never graduate.

If a man will begin in certainties he shall end in doubts; but if he will be content to begin in doubts he shall end in certainties.

—FRANCIS BACON

omer, astrophysicist, cosmologist, and science popularizer. I was honored to make a presentation on his behalf at the Cleveland Museum of Natural History when his plane was grounded by fog at his home base of Cornell University.

Sagan declared that "extraordinary claims require extraordinary evidence." All religions search for hard evidence for their extraordinary claims, but there is not one iota, jot, or tittle of support for their claims that would hold up in the court of common sense and reason.

The Christian Bible is annually the best-selling, most-stolen, and least-read book in this country. The Bible is composed of both the Old and New Testaments, so you can't believe one without the other. We are all familiar with the "good parts" of the good book, but to many the older testament is a grim fairy tale, with the ruthless slaying of innocent children, the unconditional approval of slavery, and the subjugation of women (Women are forbidden to speak in church). Throw in the right to kill your neighbor if you find him working on the Sabbath and divine approval to slay your children if they disobey you.

Modern religionists increasingly reject the ultra-religionist zealots with their arrogance, bigotry, and claims of moral superiority. Religious faith is a miraculous thing in itself, although Mark Twain allowed that "faith is believing what you know ain't so."

An outstanding example of religious faith is shown by many athletes who accomplish something and then point to the sky, thanking some supernatural being for helping with their earthly achievement. The first prominent athlete to thank an unseen celestial entity was Herb Lusk of the Philadelphia Eagles, in 1976. After scoring a touchdown, Lusk knelt prayerfully in the end zone and gave thanks. Lusk became known as the "praying tailback," and he was the progenitor of the sky-pointers who have proliferated over the years.

Perhaps the chief sky-pointer today is home run–hitting Albert Pujols of the St. Louis Cardinals, who knows that someone upstairs loves baseball—in spite of all the more important events taking place on Earth.

Contrary to popular belief, our nation was NOT founded on belief in a biblical God. Our founding fathers were Deists. Thomas Jefferson did not believe in the divinity of Jesus Christ, but he did believe in the attributes of the benevolent and loving messiah. Jefferson dismissed all the miracles of the Christian Bible, saying that they were the contrivances of mere man. Jefferson created his own Bible (I have a copy) minus the miracles that were actually claimed

" SURE GLAD I DIDN'T SMOKE, DRINK, OR FOOL AROUND. I WOULDN'T WANT TO HAVE MISSED OUT ON ALL OF THIS!"

by more than twenty "messiahs" before the Christian version. As a result, Jefferson ridiculed the clergy and had no use for them.

Abraham Lincoln, according to his law-partner colleague, William Herndon, with whom he shared the last twenty-three years of his life, was not a Christian. Herndon said our sixteenth president—who never joined a church—believed in "fate and providence." Lincoln enjoyed telling jokes about the clergy and, as a young man, wrote a scathing article mocking Christianity—which was soon torn up and destroyed by his friends. They realized that by showing contempt for the Bible he could never achieve political success (Indeed, no politician could ever advance without showing religious piety).

You will likely be surprised to know those who have professed no belief in religion. Following is a partial list of doubters, skeptics, freethinkers, secular humanists, agnostics, and atheists:

Albert Einstein, Jacques Cousteau, Mark Twain, James Baldwin, Luther Burbank, Thomas Edison, Ron Reagan, Jr., Robert Frost, Ted Turner, Larry King, Katharine Hepburn, Angelina Jolie, Jack Nicholson, Richard Leakey, Sean Penn, Warren Buffett, Billy Joel, John Lennon, Andy Rooney, Penn Jillette, Peter Ustinov, George Clooney, Howard Stern, Susan B. Anthony, Meryl Streep, Carl Sagan, Bill Gates, Barbara Walker, Richard Branson, James Taylor, John Gielgud, George Carlin, Matt Dillon, Ray Bradbury, Rick Rickards, Emily Dickinson, Clarence Darrow, Richard Dawkins, Isaac Asimov, Irving Berlin, Wolfgang Mozart, Yip Harburg, Richard Rodgers, Georges Bizet, Cole Porter, Stephen Sondheim, Scott Joplin, Jerome Kern, George Gershwin, Richard Strauss, Maurice Ravel, Hector Berlioz, Johannes Brahms, Aaron Copland, Dan Barker, Giuseppe Verdi, Napoleon Bonaparte, George Washington, Thomas Jefferson, James Monroe, John Adams, Will and Ariel Durant, Benjamin Franklin, Bill Maher, Charles Darwin.

Holiday cheer was shared at Tim Taylor's by Fox 8 pals and alums including, clockwise from me, Tony Rizzo, John Telich, Dick Russ, Lynn Zele, Joe Benny, and Loree Vick.

While no one knows for certain why we are here, many of us are hoping for some theme-park-in-the-sky. I believe—as did Mary Ann Evans so many

I'm an interdenominational skeptic; I believe Humpty Dumpty was pushed!

years ago—that the only reason any of us have for living is to make life less difficult for others. My religion is to be generous, be honest, be caring, be compassionate, and to be loving to all living things (even though I must give a wink to my favorite poet, Ogden Nash, who mused, "God in his wisdom made the fly, but then forgot to tell us why").

It was author Henry James who summed up the three things in human life that are important: The first is to be kind. The second is to be kind. And the third is to be kind.

Amen.

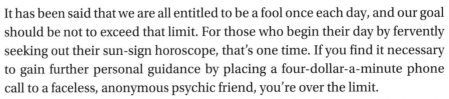

Astrologers & Psychics

If it was so, it might be;
and if it were so, it would be;
but as it isn't, it ain't.

—Tweedledee, in Lewis Carroll's *Through the Looking Glass*

It has been said that we are all entitled to be a fool once each day, and our goal should be not to exceed that limit. For those who begin their day by fervently seeking out their sun-sign horoscope, that's one time. If you find it necessary to gain further personal guidance by placing a four-dollar-a-minute phone call to a faceless, anonymous psychic friend, you're over the limit.

Do not confuse the science of astronomy with the fantasy world of astrology. Consider the *Oxford English Dictionary* definitions:

Astronomy: The science that deals with the material universe beyond Earth's atmosphere.

Astrology: The supposed art which assumes and professes to foretell the influences of celestial objects on human affairs.

Although astrology has no basis in fact, astrologers claim that the movement and positioning of a tiny number of stars—among the trillions that exist—will determine one's destiny on Earth.

"IF YOU'D BEEN BORN TWO DAYS EARLIER, YOU'D BE CHARMING, WITTY AND WISE."

Surveys in the United States have shown that one out of every four of us believes in astrology, and one-third think that sun-sign astrology is an actual science. Horoscopes are carried by two out of three newspapers. In this country there are an estimated twenty thousand astrologers with millions of disciples who spend countless millions of dollars supporting the celestial nonsense.

Astrology, denounced by the early Christian church as "a disease, not a science," is the fastest-growing belief system in the United States. In France, there are more astrologers than there are members of the Roman Catholic clergy.

Astrology was born some four thousand years ago in ancient Babylonia (now Iraq) when superstition and magic ruled and the earth was thought to be the center of the universe around which all heavenly bodies circled. Early civilizations were in awe of the objects in the nighttime sky, but they had no way of knowing the immensity of the universe and the tremendous physical distances between the stars and the planets. The stars that made up the constellations were believed to be nearby neighbors and on the same horizontal plane. The ancients did not realize that those bright suns were billions and trillions of miles away from each other. (For this reason you could never take a trip to the constellation Orion, for example. As you approached the nearest star in Orion, the familiar pattern, as seen from Earth, would become unrecognizable and simply disappear.)

The ancient priests, who had no calendar, laid the groundwork for astrology when they relied on observation of stars and star patterns to guide their people through the seasons. In order to keep their power and control,

This 1980 photo is my claim to fame with an astronaut as well as proof that I was young once, too. The man in the hat is Wally Schirra, one of NASA's original Mercury 7 astronauts and the only person to fly in the first three space programs, Mercury, Gemini, and Apollo. It was a lucky encounter on the beach in Maui, Hawaii.

DICK'S MEMORIES

Bad Period

I've been invited to speak to many organizations. Upon leaving Fox 8 one evening, I grabbed an empty box in the storeroom into which I put my weather guides. Arriving late, I walked down the long center aisle and was surprised by the chuckles and laughter en route. Only later did I learn that the box I had snatched had the word KOTEX emblazoned in large gothic letters on it.

*The greatness of a
nation and its moral
progress can be judged
by the way its animals
are treated.*

—MOHANDUS K. GHANDI

Each year I have the honor of
crowning the Woollybear King and
Woollybear Queen.

the priests eventually proclaimed an ability to divine the fate of kings and
the growth of crops and predict famines, war, catastrophes, and the weather.
Personal predictions—individual birth horoscopes—date from after the thir-
teenth century B.C. The horoscopes were developed by the astrologer's observation of the sun, moon, and planets (technically, even the sun and moon are
considered planets by astrologers) in relation to the background star constellations at the time of birth. (Wouldn't the time of conception be a more valid
starting point?) The constellations were divided into twelve large regions of
the heavens called the zodiac, which cover the sky like elongated tiles. (The
word *zodiac* comes from the Greek *zodiakos kyklos,* which means "circle of
animals." There are eighty-eight constellations that are observable from Earth,
and the dozen that make up the signs of the zodiac were finalized in the eighth
century B.C.)

The ancients saw pictures in the nighttime sky, and observing the star con-
figurations that make up the zodiac, we must conclude that they had vivid
imaginations. As you look at the random star clusters, you can make up your
own zodiacal mandala of animals or mythological heroes. Connect the imagi-
nary lines and Sagittarius could be a spider, Pisces a cat, and so forth.

While astrologers purport that stars exert a profound influence on the human body and mind, the distances from the earth to the stars are so great
that any possible gravitational, vibrational, or magnetic attraction or effect is
minuscule. Studies have shown not one scintilla of correlation between the
positions and motions of heavenly objects and the lives of human beings. The
astrologer will also impute to each planet and constellation the ability to represent a different facet of the human personality. For example, the red planet
Mars, which rules the sign of Aries, supposedly exemplifies aggression and
war, and, so goes the absurdity, produces the world's greatest athletes. Con-
versely, the watery planet Neptune governs the sign Pisces. Pisceans are considered indecisive and weak, often daydreaming away their opportunities.

A major problem with astrology—and most astrologers will not tell you
this—is the scientific fact called the precession of the equinoxes. Because
Earth wobbles on its axis as it rotates in its orbit around the sun, the zodia-

What do we live for if it is not to make life less difficult for each other?

—GEORGE ELIOT (MARY ANN EVANS)

cal signs have actually moved one whole sign backward over the last two thousand years. It will be another 23,800 years before the precessional cycle returns to its original starting point. Some two thousand years ago, at the time of the vernal equinox, the sun was "in" the constellation Aries, while today it is "in" Pisces. This means that although I was born on the 24th day of February, I'm not a weak, wishy-washy Pisces after all. Instead, I'm a militant, dominating Aquarian. (I know this must be so; otherwise, I couldn't have written this.)

I wore my original U.S. Air Force uniform to sing the national anthem at a Memorial Day observance near Akron.

It would be too easy to say that astrology is simply a myth agreed upon because astrologers, when presented with identical sun-sign charts, frequently disagree on what the chart forecasts. One of the most widely published astrologers has complained that at least one-half of his fellow stargazers are charlatans who have no idea what they are doing. But the business of astrology is a highly profitable enterprise, and the most advanced practitioners will run up the bill by dazzling their clients with such exotic concepts as "quincunx," "quintile," "sextile," "medium coeli," and "sesquiquad-rate."

It's easy to see why so many believe in astrology. When we find our sun sign, we compare the sign's characteristics to what we believe about ourselves. Personal traits often listed among the sun signs are: cautious, extroverted, introverted, insecure, confident, passive, aggressive, adventurous, sensitive, considerate, intuitive, authoritative, compassionate, aloof, and forthright. Who wouldn't qualify for several, if not most, of those traits, at least occasionally? We also remember the ones that we feel fit our personality and forget the rest.

Basically, astrology operates under the philosophy that if you throw enough mud (there's a better word) at a wall, some of it is going to stick.

Life is a (excrement) sandwich and every day we take another bite.

While the science of astronomy has made gigantic progress over the millennia, the pseudoscience of astrology remains stuck in the desert sand of its birthplace. Astrology has not changed in two thousand years. Its main contribution to humanity is that "What's your sign?" is second only to "Do you come here often?" as the classic social icebreaker.

If a dog will not come to you after he has looked you in the face, you should go home and examine your conscience.

—WOODROW WILSON

Changing Signs

Because of the idiosyncrasies of the earth's orbit around the sun, the stars do not match up with their allotted zodiac months. For example, the sun no longer appears in the constellation, or house, of Aries in March and early April. It makes its annual flyby in mid-April and early May. There is an additional constellation that the sun passes through in December, and this zodiac sign is known as Ophiuchus, the snake-bearer. Hisssss. If this irritates you, remember that the zodiac is based on the seasons, so we can all return to our original signs!

Sagittarius: December 17–January 20
Capricorn: January 20–February 16
Aquarius: February 16–March 11
Pisces: March 11–April 18
Aries: April 18–May 13
Taurus: May 13–June 21
Gemini: June 21–July 20
Cancer: July 20–August 10
Leo: August 10–September 16
Virgo: September 16–October 30
Libra: October 30–November 23
Scorpio: November 23–November 29
Ophiuchus: November 29–December 17

"WHY DO I NEED A HUSBAND? I'VE GOT A STOVE THAT SMOKES, A BIRD THAT SWEARS, AND A CAT THAT STAYS OUT ALL NIGHT."

Psychics

While astrology, if not taken seriously, can be entertaining, there can be no redemption for the fortune-telling media psychics. The phony psychic networks are raking in an estimated $400 million a year by preying upon the most gullible, most vulnerable, and least affluent among us. Fronted and promoted on television by down-on-their-luck entertainers, this scam thrives because, as in astrology, the will to believe overwhelms common sense.

In search of an accurate five-day forecast, I called a psychic pal on the four-

The brook would lose its song if the rocks were removed.

DICK'S PALS

Feed the Birds

JEFF COLLINS: You know how Dick always says, "Feed the birds" in the winter? He doesn't just say it. When I worked at a garden supply store in Bay Village, back in the mid-1980s, he was in every week, buying tons of bird seed, so he's doing it, too. Everybody looked forward to when he came in.

We had a couple of barn cats in the store, and the owner didn't like having them around. They did keep down the mice that we had with all those grains, but the owner was afraid they'd have kittens, and he didn't want that. He said it was our responsibility to get them fixed.

Dick was in the store. When the boss left, he walked up to the counter and said he overheard. He said, "Take them to a vet. I'll take care of it." And he handed me a blank check to cover it.

When we'd have a flea dip for pets, he'd always announce it on TV.

He came in with a new car once and backed it up to the back door to load the bird feed. I needed to move a truck and asked him to pull out. He tossed me the keys to the car and said, "Take it out and see what you think." Just like that.

He was totally cool. You meet some people who are on TV or radio and they're arrogant, they're cocky. You don't get any of that from Dick. Totally real. Totally cool.

Jeff Collins is director of maintenance at the Cuyahoga County Fairgrounds and keeper of its apiary.

Roker on Goddard

MARK DAWIDZIAK: Al Roker is a native New Yorker, but he was so embraced and popular as Channel 3's chief weather anchor from 1978 to 1983 that a lot of people still think he's a Clevelander. I once asked him what it was like competing with Dick Goddard. "I wasn't Dick Goddard's competition," he said. "I was just in the same market at the same time. Cleveland was Dick Goddard's town, and still is."

Mark Dawidziak has covered television in Cleveland since 1983 as a critic for the Beacon Journal *and now the* Plain Dealer.

Men will be just to men when they are kind to animals.

—HENRY BERGH

My own bobblehead, made by Bosley Bobbers of Louisville, Ohio. They've also made bobblehead dolls of Abraham Lincoln, Al Capone, and Albert Einstein. A warehouse fire in 2009 destroyed most of my bobbleheads, which have become hard-to-find collector's items.

"REMINDS ME OF THE BLIZZARD OF 2072!"

The probability that someone is watching you is in direct proportion to the stupidity of what you are doing.

—MORRIS BENDER

dollars-a-minute 800 telephone number. My new best friend said that her name was "Star" and in a pleasant voice began to elicit information from me, including (curiously?) my astrological sun sign. The technique Star was using is known to professional psychologists as a "cold reading," which meant that the information I had given would soon be returned to me in such a way that I was supposed to be amazed at her clairvoyance.

Just as in astrology, pseudopsychics such as Star are schooled in the fact that people are basically more alike than different. We all share common problems and concerns, and the charlatan soothsayers are very happy to tell us what we want to hear.

The ability to keep the telephone money meter running is a prerequisite for electronic psychics, so as the twenty-minute, eighty-dollar mark approached, I reluctantly informed my glib buddy that it was time that I faced the future on my own. At that point I confessed that I, too, was a prominent psychic, and that I could see a handsome and wealthy man entering her life. As she asked for details, I regretted that I had run out of time and politely hung up.

While psychic abilities may exist (Haven't we all, seemingly, "been in this place before"?), there is no conclusive, decisive proof. The problem with both astrologers and psychics is that Western law regards both as simple fortune-tellers. Under our treasured freedom of speech, such hokum and flimflam are not illegal and are viewed only as entertainment, as if both were harmless. Unfortunately, too many people forfeit their free will, rationality, and sense of personal responsibility by resigning their fate to the idea that "if it's in the stars, there's nothing I can do about it."

I am personally aware of one bankruptcy that can be blamed on psychic readings, and, nationally, there has been at least one documented suicide.

It's an Illusion

In ancient times it was believed that the earth—not the sun—was the center of the universe, and the stars continually raced around our planet. It wasn't until the sixteenth century that the Polish astronomer Nicholas Copernicus proved that the sun was the center of our world.

Stars, because of their enormous distances from Earth, remain stationary, but due to Earth's counterclockwise rotation, they seem to move across the sky from east to west. The sun, moon, and all other celestial bodies also give the ILLUSION of moving from east to west. Planets, unlike stars, have no fixed locations and continually change positions on our sky.

....

Take a Lot of Sandwiches

A light year is the distance light travels—at 186,282 miles per second—through space. Thus, a particle of light will, in one year, travel 5,878,000,000,000 (nearly six trillion) miles.

The nearest star to Earth, except for the sun, is Proxima Centauri, some 4.3 light years away. Only powerful telescopes can see this distant sun.

The nearest star that can be seen with the naked eye is the brilliant Sirius (the Dog Star). Do not confuse Sirius with the planets Venus, Mars, and Jupiter, which are relatively close to Earth. Sirius is nine light years from our planet (53 trillion miles). Don't expect Neil Zurcher to include Sirius in a One Tank Trip. In a spaceship traveling 50,000 miles per hour, it would take over 100,000 years to reach Sirius.

....

Whatever Goes Around, Etc.

Along with planet Earth, there are eight other planets, sixty-five known moons, and countless comets and asteroids orbiting the sun. After forty years of space launches, the U.S. Air Force is also tracking about eight thousand pieces of man-made space debris.

To successfully launch a spacecraft into orbit, two opposing forces must be in perfect balance: (1) gravity (continually pulling objects downward), and (2) force of inertia (which makes objects travel a straight line, unless pulled off course). At a speed of about 5 miles per second (18,000 miles per hour), the two forces equalize and objects will remain forever in orbit unless something slows them down or speeds them up (a spacecraft rocket booster, for example).

Hard work never killed a man, but it sure has scared a lot of them.

My buddies. We did two Las Vegas tours and made sure we had proof. Clockwise from me are Tim Taylor, Lil' John Rinaldi, Big Chuck Schodowski, and Fox 8 morning reporter Kenny Crumpton.

Unimaginably Immense

On very clear nights the sky seems to be carpeted by countless stars, with from two- to three thousand visible to the naked eye. In reality, however, those fiery suns we call stars are millions, billions, and trillions of miles apart. Visualize a few dozen baseballs scattered across the United States and you will have an idea of the distance between stars.

More incredibly, if the universe were a building twenty miles long, twenty miles wide, and twenty miles high, all the matter within the cosmos would be no larger than a single grain of sand.

Chicken Little Time

Comets and asteroids are visitors from deep space that rarely threaten Earth. A comet is a dirty iceberg.

Asteroids are chunks of rock and metal that range in size from a basketball to a 600-mile-wide monster known as Ceres (That's almost as broad as the state of Texas). Is there an asteroid out there headed towards Earth with our name on it? YES—and its name is Cleveland!

Here Comes Cleveland!

An asteroid is a mini-planet, and astronomers have detected and numbered about 3,300 of the hundreds of thousands that orbit the sun. While nearly all stay harmlessly within their orbits, some have occasionally broken free and roam the solar system. In June 1993, a 30-foot-wide asteroid whizzed by our planet at a distance of 90,000 miles. This bomb from outer space was not detected until it had passed!

A jury consists of twelve persons chosen to decide who has the better lawyer.

—ROBERT FROST

Dick's Partners

Dick delivered his first TV forecast on May 1, 1961, on KYW-TV3's *Eyewitness News* at noon, with anchor John "Bud" Dancy and sportscaster Jim Graner. He briefly left Cleveland for Philadelphia with KYW on June 18, 1965, and returned to local airwaves on March 28, 1966, joining WJW-TV8's *City Camera* news team, which then included news anchors Doug Adair and Joel Daly and sportscaster Ken Coleman.

These are the other primary newscasters and sportscasters on Dick's Cleveland anchor teams since 1961:

Those who marry for money earn every cent of it.

Hugh Danaceau (TV3)	Denise D'Ascenzo	Fred McLeod
Bill Jorgensen (TV3)	Denise Dufala	Jim Mueller
Pat Murray (TV3)	John FitzGerald	Tony Rizzo
Tom Snyder (TV3)	Frank Glieber	Marty Ross
Carl Stern (TV3)	Jim Hale	Marty Savidge
Stacy Bell	Judd Hambrick	Wilma Smith
Tana Carli	Lou Maglio	Murray Stewart
Vince Cellini	Bill Martin	Robin Swoboda
Casey Coleman	Dave Martin	John Telich
Dan Coughlin	Jeff Maynor	Tim Taylor

Left: The mid-1970s anchor desk at TV8 featured sportscaster Jim Mueller, newscasters Jim Hale and Jeff Maynor, and me.

Right: TV8's *City Camera* anchor team ending the 1960s featured, from left, Marty Ross and Doug Adair, sportscaster Dave Martin and me.

DICK'S PALS

CERTIFIED POPULAR

Dick was rated as the most popular weathercaster in America in a national survey of newscaster popularity conducted by Herb Altman Communications in the late 1980s.

Readers and editors of *Cleveland Magazine* voted for Dick as "Best Weatherperson" in the magazine's annual "Best Of" issue in September 2008.

The January 2001 edition of *Ohio Magazine* named him "Ohio's Best Meteorologist" in its January 2001 edition.

Great Save

ROBIN SWOBODA: I was seated across from the general manager. Dick was to my right on a sofa, and Tim was next to him. Casey Coleman and Virgil Dominic, who was news director, were at the end.

The general manager would get tongue-tied. He was explaining what Channel 3 was doing, sandwiching the network news between local. He got hung up on "sandwiching."

I started to laugh and put my head down. I heard Dick exhaling from his nose, so I knew he was laughing. I saw Tim and Casey not cracking a smile, holding it, which made me laugh even harder. I was convulsing. Suddenly Dick jumped up and said, "Look, a flock of honkers!"

He saved us and saved the GM. Nobody's ever laughed harder about a flock of geese.

Off the Chart

KEVIN SALYER: Back in the '80s and into the '90s, when we'd have news consultants come in, they always were stunned to see how incredibly popular Dick was. If you're not from around here, you don't get it. I remember one of these guys pointing at the top of a screen and saying, "Now, your big-time guys are here." Then he put his hand way over the top of the screen, in the air, and said, "Dick Goddard is here." That's how you explain Dick's popularity in this area. He's off the chart.

Kevin Salyer, WJW's vice president for programming and promotion, grew up watching the station, where he has now worked for three decades.

DICK'S MEMORIES

He Shoots, He Scores

Wilma Smith hosted a new program at Fox 8, and as guests she had a father and son. She unveiled a hockey game in which she played goalie. After the event, I announced to viewers what they had just seen: the father, the son, and the goalie host. One very upset minister called to secure my destiny in that fiery furnace.

GLOBAL WARMING

In October of 1997 many whose job it was to forecast the weather on television were summoned to the White House in an attempt to win over meteorologists to the proposition that climate change resulting from global warming was a reality, not just a theory. The event got off to a shaky start.

....

As about one hundred of us—including high-ranking officials from National Oceanic and Atmospheric Administration, the National Weather Service, and the American Meteorological Society—were waiting in a long security-check line outside the White House, it began to rain. And not one of us had an umbrella! (If a major tabloid had had their weatherazzi on hand, we would have been a drop-dead cinch to make the next day's front page under a banner headline exclaiming, "Weather Fools Meet the President.")

In the East Room, President Clinton made a brief, cordial welcoming speech. We all knew the president was setting the table for Vice President Al Gore, who has made global warming a personal crusade. For nearly an hour the vice president made what I thought was an impressive and compelling presentation, complete with graphs and pie charts. The problem was that the majority of meteorologists who had come to the conference were unconvinced that global warming is real, and they went away with the same opinion.

In reality we are passengers on a spaceship called Earth that circles a life-giving star we call our sun. However we view our earthly home, there is little scientific doubt that because of neglect and poor housekeeping we have be-

You know your children are growing up when they stop asking you where they come from and refuse to tell you where they're going.

—P. J. O'ROURKE

Top: Don Webster seems to be watching in concern at the White House as I give a woollybear sticker to President Bill Clinton, at a climate-change conference for television forecasters in 1997.

Bottom: The woollybear sticker didn't make the photo, but I did give one to Vice President Al Gore at a 1997 White House conference on climate change for about a hundred TV weather forecasters.

fouled our own nest. Fortunately, planet Earth has a remarkable ability to heal itself. The question is, just how much can it handle?

While core samples of glacial ice tell a story of dramatic changes in the earth's climate over millions of years, these changes have very likely come from such disparate things as collisions with comets and asteroids or the eccentric wobbling of our planet on its axis. It wasn't until the beginning of the Industrial Revolution that human beings acquired the ability to change the climate and damage our finely tuned ecosystem. Our power to alter the atmosphere cannot be minimized.

Pollution can be environmental (natural) or anthropogenic (man-made), and it can occur in our air, land, and water. An example of natural pollution is a volcanic eruption; the burning of fossil fuels (coal, petroleum, and natural gas) in factories, automobile engines, and home furnaces is an example of man-made contamination.

It was estimated that over this century that the concentration of carbon dioxide—caused primarily by the burning of fossil fuels—was 25 percent higher than at the start of the century. Those who deny that there is any current global warming point to the fact that, with the earth 71 percent water-covered, the oceans act as colossal "sinks," absorbing excessive carbon dioxide and thus keeping the climate in balance.

The warming of Earth's climate has been labeled the "greenhouse effect", although "hothouse effect" or "heat trap effect" would be equally appropriate. Short-wavelength sunlight easily passes through a greenhouse's glass, while the absorbed sunlight within is then reradiated as long-wavelength radiation, which the greenhouse glass blocks from escaping. Correspondingly, Earth's atmosphere is almost transparent to incoming sunlight, but carbon dioxide gas traps much of the infrared heat energy that is reradiated from our planet.

Scientists recognize carbon dioxide as the largest single contributor to the greenhouse effect over the past century, but the cumulative effect of nitrogen oxides, methane, ozone, chlorofluorocarbons, and other trace gases could equal that of carbon dioxide over this century.

Aside from fossil fuel burning, which produces more carbon dioxide than any other activity, deforestation of the earth's surface has been the largest single source of this gas. Trees absorb carbon dioxide, and when they die and rot they unlock and release the gas back into the atmosphere. (Planting new trees is one method of reducing carbon dioxide accumulation.)

Methane, a gas that emanates from landfills, the digestive tracts of cattle, termite mounds, and rice patties, also contributes to the greenhouse effect. Improved landfill procedures and new methods of managing cattle and growing rice are being examined by environmentalists.

Love makes the world go round, but laughter keeps us from getting dizzy.

Computer estimates suggest that with a dramatic greenhouse effect, the layer of air from the earth's surface to twelve miles aloft would warm, while the stratospheric layer above would cool. Earth's higher latitudes (including Ohio's) would warm, while the tropics would show little change. There would be catastrophic drought in grain-producing latitudes (including ours) while some now drought-plagued areas would get abundant rainfall. Glaciers and ice caps would melt, and the rise in ocean water levels would inundate present-day coastal regions.

To this scenario the global warming skeptics say, "No!" They claim that the supercomputer projections are flawed, and they reject the idea that surface temperature observations over the last decades are accurate. Satellite observa-

Glaciers and ice caps would melt.

tions have actually shown no change, or even a lowering of temperatures. Many respected climatologists believe that any global warming (or cooling) is a natural phenomenon, and that variations in global temperatures have come in cycles over extremely long periods of time. A 1997 survey of climatologists in the United States revealed that 58 percent did not believe there is overwhelming evidence that global warming is for real. In contrast, 36 percent agreed with the global warming theory. Curiously, about 36 percent of climatologists believe that Earth is headed for another glacial period.

I believe such skepticism is healthy, if it is maintained in an altruistic spirit with the search for truth as its goal. I have a file from the 1960s packed with

It is never too soon to be kind, for we never know how soon it will be too late.

—GRACE SIMPSON, MT. JULIET, TENNESSEE

Left to right: Doug Adair, Marty Ross, Dick Goddard, Dave Martin.

magazine and newspaper articles warning that the next ice age was closing in, rapidly. With just as much zeal as today's advocates of global warming theory, the ice-age people were issuing a clarion call for immediate action if the coming deep freeze was to be somehow ameliorated (one suggestion was to spread lampblack over polar regions to absorb solar radiation and melt the ice sheets).

By the late 1970s, the frigorific forecasts suddenly disappeared and, following a brief climatological interregnum, the hothouse people emerged with their own reading of the global thermostat. During the 1997 White House conference on global warming I found a great opportunity to quiz two respected meteorologists on the subject. I told them about my three-inch-thick file from the 1960s and asked, "Where did the ice-age people go?" The National Weather Service official smiled broadly and poked his finger at the American Meteorological Society member next to him. The pokee, who was obviously very sensitive to the question, returned a less-than-broad smile and a shrug.

Actually, life on Earth can be adversely affected by many unpredictable events:

EARTH'S ORBIT around the sun ranges from elliptical to nearly circular, and it recycles about every 100,000 years. Earth's current 23.5-degree tilt on its axis will range between 22 and 24 degrees, a considerable variance.

SOLAR VARIABILITY changes with incoming radiation rising and falling with sunspot activity (storms on the sun). This effect is ancient and extremely changeable, affecting not only the temperature on Earth, but the amount of ozone and rainfall.

COMETS AND ASTEROIDS (miniplanets) have bombarded Earth over the eons, creating enormous tsunamis (incorrectly called tidal waves) and life-threatening, sunlight-blocking ash and dust clouds. Earth's orbit and the tilt of its axis could be affected.

VOLCANOES can spread ash around the planet, shutting off sunlight and causing the earth's temperature to drop dramatically. The Year Without a

Summer (1816) was caused by the eruption of Mount Tambora in Indonesia in 1815.

SHIFTING OF EARTH'S TECTONIC PLATES can rearrange its geography, which would change weather patterns.

NUCLEAR WAR, with its resultant clouds and radiation, could theoretically create a life-destroying "nuclear winter."

We have no right, of course, to be in high (or even low) dudgeon when nature, which created this planet, decides to do some rearranging. In truth, beautiful planet Earth, hanging like a bright blue sapphire in the blackness of space, and embellished with majestic mountains and seas, is hostile. Created in the unimaginable violence of an exploding and (perhaps) ever-expanding universe some 4.6 billion years ago, tilted and wobbling as it circles the sun, the earth is wracked by an earthquake every ten minutes. Dust from volcanoes is constantly in our atmosphere, while ice ages have advanced and retreated.

But those of us alive today should be most thankful. In the lottery of life, twentieth and twenty-first century Americans drew some very good numbers. Through modern science and the Industrial Revolution, we have been given a prosperous, artificial way of life, shielded from much of nature's violence. Through no effort of our own, and in spite of highly publicized heat waves, blizzards, tsunamis, hurricanes, and tornadoes, the climate of the last fifty years has smiled benignly on the United States. Some climatologists have concluded that since the end of the Dust Bowl days of the 1930s, we have been blessed with the mildest and most agriculturally productive weather in the last ten thousand years. What we have perceived as "normal" weather has instead been at the most favorable extreme possible.

When the people fear the government, we have tyranny. When the government fears the people, we have liberty.

—UNKNOWN (THOUGH SOMETIMES ATTRIBUTED TO THOMAS JEFFERSON)

DICK'S MEMORIES

Babe Watch

The most-watched TV show of all time—1.1 billion viewers worldwide—was the 1990s *Baywatch*. Men were the target audience for the flimsy storylines about Los Angeles County lifeguards, who were mainly young ladies patrolling the beaches in their equally flimsy bikinis. I took the call from an enraged young man who complained that our stupid weather warnings were "covering up the best parts."

DICK'S PALS

Fishin' with Dick

"BIG CHUCK" SCHODOWSKI: Dick's protection of animal life got him involved in things I didn't expect. For instance, although most of the *Big Chuck & Lil' John* and *Hoolihan and Big Chuck* skits were pretty much my own ideas, a great number were derived from jokes. One such joke went like this:

A Catholic priest was trying to get one of his parishioners to quit drinking. He asked him to come to the parish house one night to have a chat. When the man arrived, the priest sat him down next to his desk and pointed out that on the desk were two drinking glasses. One was filled with fresh drinking water, and the other was filled with gin. He then opened a container of earthworms, took one out, and said, "Watch what happens when I put the worm into the glass of water. See how the worm swims around enjoying the cool, fresh water?" Taking another worm out of the container, he told the man, "Now watch what happens when I put this worm into the demon alcohol." Within seconds, the worm in the gin shriveled up and died. "There!" said the priest. "Did you see that? Now what lesson does that teach you?"

Did you see that? Now what lesson does that teach you?

"A very good lesson, Father," the parishioner responded. "If you drink booze, you'll never get worms."

I scheduled studio time and crew, scripted the skit and camera shots, built the office set, got costumes, and round up the props—two clear glasses, a water pitcher, a bottle of gin, and, oh yes, live worms. I have always prided myself on being thoroughly prepared for a shoot, thinking of things that could go wrong, and having a backup plan in case of emergency.

Tape time was set for a Tuesday, 7:30 to 9 p.m. I had the props ready at the studio, everything but the live worms. At about 5 p.m., I went to a bait shop just around the corner from TV8 and bought a dozen worms. Everything was ready. So I went to our cafeteria to get a sandwich to eat while I watched our six o'clock news. During a commercial break, I began to go over production details. I opened the container of worms to make sure they were alive and active. They were.

Then it hit me like a ton of bricks—I needed one dead worm. I didn't have a dead worm. I began to panic, but then I thought, no problem,

OH, DOCTOR, IT WAS TERRIBLE... THERE I WAS, SURROUNDED BY THESE GIANT ORANGE AND BLACK CATERPILLAR LARVA!

I'll kill one. But how? I began to panic again. I'll cut off his head, I thought. But I've seen worms completely cut in half while fishing, and both ends stay alive. I decided to smash it but realized that would be too messy and the worm wouldn't look right. Oh, man! It was about thirty minutes to tape time, and I thought, what the hell am I going to do? How am I going to kill a worm without destroying its body? Then I glanced down at my sandwich and a light bulb went on in my head—the cafeteria has three microwaves! I'll nuke the worm!

I felt very relieved and very guilty at the same time. I had never deliberately executed anything in my life. But, as they say, the show must go on. I had to hurry. It was about 6:45 p.m., the news would be over at 7 p.m., and the entire shift would be in the cafeteria to eat lunch two minutes later.

I grabbed the worms, ran down the hall, and peeked into the cafeteria. Perfect. No one was there. My heart was beating faster and faster. I began to feel like a ghoul, about to do something very unnatural to satisfy my selfish needs. "This is not for me," I told myself. "It's for my craft!"

As I placed a worm on a paper plate, another question hit me. How long do you nuke a worm to kill it? I decided to try fifteen seconds. I pressed the start button and began to think of all the old prison movies I had seen as a kid, with the prison guard throwing the switch on the electric chair. I felt really creepy.

I looked out the cafeteria door as the microwave buzzed away. No one in sight. Good! It was the longest fifteen seconds of my life, but it was over. I took the paper plate out of the microwave and gasped in shock. The worm was gone. I looked all over inside the microwave. No worm in sight. Then I noticed what looked like a very faint S-shaped pencil line on the plate. It was the worm. Vaporized. Obviously, fifteen seconds was too long. I grabbed another worm, set the timer for ten seconds, and "zap." This time, I didn't feel as guilty. When I took out the paper plate, the worm looked more like an "S" drawn with a crayon. I looked at my watch. It was two minutes to seven o'clock. The news was over and the crews would soon be in the cafeteria.

I had one more shot. Would five seconds be enough? No. Still too much. Three seconds? Not enough? I was fast running out of time—and worms, for that matter. I put a new worm in, set the timer for three seconds, zapped, opened the door, and there it was—a perfectly formed worm, dead as a doornail. Whew! It worked.

I grabbed the plate and container of worms and turned to leave—only to find

Actor and producer Michael Douglas had two Oscars and two Golden Globes, so I made sure he had a woollybear sticker to give him the triple crown.

Accept that some days you're the pigeon and some days you're the statue.

—ROGER C. ANDERSON

My daughter, Kim, on stage with me at the Woollybear Festival and (below) with her Rottweilers, Bunnie and Peace.

Linda Norman from the camera crew looking down at my plate. "What is that?" she asked. "Is that a worm? What did you do with it?" I tried to think of a believable lie, but drew a blank. "I . . . ah . . . I put it in the microwave." "What!?" she gasped. "You're gross! Why did you do a horrible thing like that?"

"I need it for a skit," I said, and started to leave because others were coming in. She yelled, "Wait! Which microwave did you use? I don't want to use that one."

"I'm not telling you," I teased, and started down the hallway. "You called me gross!"

"You'd better tell me!" she yelled back. "Or—or I'm going to tell Dick Goddard what you did!"

That really got my attention. But, I figured, what's done is done, no turning back now. We did the skit, and it turned out great. The acting, the special effects, everything was excellent—even the worms.

The next day, when I got to work, a brown paper bag with a note attached was on my desk. I immediately noticed the signature at the bottom, "Dick Goddard," and I knew Linda had blown the whistle on me. "Charlie," the note read, "Next time you need worms for a skit, use these." In the bag was an assortment of plastic worms. To the day I retired, I kept that bag of worms in our prop room as a reminder of the heinous act perpetrated in the name of showbiz.

I later saw a picture of Dick as a young boy on our news show's baby picture quiz segment. He was holding a fishing pole, and I thought, "What did Dick do to the worms he used as bait?" A funny line came to me, one that we still use in our stand-up routine in live shows: "You know, people always ask us, 'Is Dick Goddard as nice as everyone says?' Well, folks, Dick truly is Mr. Nice Guy, and, believe me, he is the biggest animal lover on the planet. For instance, whenever Dick goes fishing he tapes the worms to his hook."

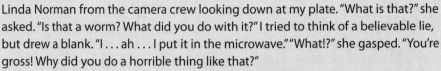

DICK'S MEMORIES

Here Comes Jack Lord

One year in the mid-1990s we were doing the Thanksgiving weekend parade, which the station sponsored in downtown Cleveland. Evidently we didn't have the rights to some Christmas music, so every time a unit went by that required that music, we played the theme from *Hawaii 5-0*. That was a highlight. "Here comes Santa Claus—and the theme from Jack Lord and *Hawaii 5-0!*"

When Your Tang Gets Toungled

They are called spoonerisms, and it's fair to say that anyone who has the power of speech has fallen prey to this type of linguistic transposition. Those who chronically suffer from the mixing up of words are the victims of what is known as metathesis. Fortunately, metathesis is not fatal, although its victims sometimes feel as if they are about to die of embarrassment. There is also no cure for this affliction, aside from keeping your mouth shut.

TV8 was long the local affiliate for the Jerry Lewis Muscular Dystrophy Telethon on Labor Day weekend, and I frequently hosted our cut-ins. When Jerry came to town in preparation, I made sure he had a Woollybear Festival sticker.

I've spent a career butchering the King's English on Cleveland television, and I enjoy verbal somersaults as much as anyone. Three times over the years, Dick Clark's television blooper show has exposed my shortcomings. The derision of my newsroom friends turns to envy, however, when a check for eight hundred bucks shows up—at which time comes the question, "Now where do I send my tape?"

My favorite gaffe came during the Fox 8 Jerry Lewis Telethon in 1989, when it was my turn to announce our new venue, Stouffer's Tower City Plaza. It seemed like they would rename it every couple of years. Thank goodness this was very early in the morning, 5 a.m., nearing the end of a twenty-hour telethon.

They would always assign me to go down in the catacombs where there was a phone bank, and next to me was the ever-faithful and always-smiling Sister Angela. I thanked her and the volunteers, but the director was in my ear, saying, "Tell them they can come down and watch the end of the show."

If you cannot find happiness along the way, you will not find it at the end of the road.

—ANONYMOUS

When Dick Clark came to town in 1990, of course I had to give him a woollybear sticker. You can see how proud he was.

I said, "Oh, and by the way, we're down to our last couple of hours. If you would like to come down and watch the remainder of the show, we are here in a new venue—come on down to the beautiful, newly renovated Stouffer's Sour Titty Plaza."

The word *spoonerism* has come to us from the verbal misadventures of the Rev. Dr. William Archibald Spooner, who for sixty-two years was an esteemed professor, theologian, and warden (president) at New College, Oxford University in England. Dr. Spooner passed from this trail of years—make that veil of tears—in 1930 at the age of eighty-six. All who knew him agreed that he was a kindly and conscientious teacher whose only problem was that he inadvertently savaged the English language.

Perhaps the initial storm warning of his affliction came the first Sunday that he was asked to address the church congregation. Dr. Spooner mounted the pulpit and asked the elders to "please, make sure the congregation is sewn to their sheets."

Once, after introducing a church speaker, Dr. Spooner headed for his favorite spot in the pews, where he found a comely lass solidly entrenched. "Mardon me, padam," whispered Dr. Spooner, "I believe you are occupewing my pie."

As his years at Oxford multiplied, so did the spoonerisms. Students began to mimic their beleaguered professor, and eventually there arose a list of verbal blunders falsely attributed to him. By 1955, the word *spoonerisms* had been firmly established. Apocryphal or not, here is a sampling of Dr. Spooner's most precious tongue twisters:

In a speech welcoming Queen Victoria to Oxford, Dr. Spooner wanted to confide to Her Majesty that "In my bosom I have a half-formed wish," which unfortunately came out, "In my bosom I have a half-warmed fish."

Chastising a student who had wasted two academic terms and continually missed his history lectures, Spooner accused him of "not only hissing my mystery lectures, but tasting two worms."

To a miscreant who had set a fire on the Oxford campus, Spooner charged him with "fighting a liar in the Quadrangle."

Spooner augmented his speech problems with the absent-minded-professor syndrome. After a lengthy treatise to an auditorium filled with students, he suddenly realized that his train of thought had wandered off track. As he concluded his lecture he told the bemused audience that "during the presentation I have just given, whenever I said 'Aristotle,' I meant 'St. Paul.'"

Spooner once invited a man he had just met to attend a tea for a newly appointed archeology professor. "I am the new archeology professor," explained the man. "Never mind," said Spooner, "come just the same."

In everyday conversation a spoonerism is usually met with a smile or chuckle, but when the spoonerism is committed by a public figure before a large audience, the verbal gaffe will live on in perpetuity.

Anyone who has done radio or television for any length of time will pile up a steadily growing list of speaking blunders.

The late Cleveland sportscaster Jim Graner, who had Johnson's Jay Wax for a sponsor, told his listeners one evening to be sure to pick up a can of "Jackson's John Wax."

A radio station in northern Ohio directed its disc jockeys always to follow the reading of the local weather forecast with the words, "Now, let's take a look out the window." You can imagine the embarrassment of the morning jock—and the glee of his listeners—when he substituted the word *leak* for *look*.

My first experience with spoonerisms came when I worked at the Weather Bureau at Akron-Canton airport doing radio broadcasts. We were all air force or navy vets, experienced weather people, and we thought we were a big deal being on the radio. One day our boss told us we had a new sponsor. Yeah, we said, no big deal. He said, "I hope not. Your sponsor is City Chevrolet." You can't imagine how often, no matter how we got into it, we'd say, "Shitty, uh, City Chevrolet." That was my first on-air exposure to the word *city*. That one can get you in a lot of trouble.

Nature sets limits on man's wisdom, but none on his stupidity.

"MY NEXT DANCE WILL BRING LOWER DEW POINTS, RISING BAROMETRIC PRESSURE AND GRADUALLY CLEARING SKIES."

The dog has a share of man's intelligence, but none of man's falsehoods.

—SIR WALTER SCOTT

I worked all night at the Weather Bureau, and would drive back to Kent with KYW and Big Wilson on the radio. One morning he was on the air with Gloria Brown, who hosted women's shows on radio and TV for KYW. He said, "All right, Gloria, one more time, who do we write to?" She said, "Make that Betty Crooker and her cockbook . . . Oh! What did I say?" Big laughed and said, "We probably just sold a lot of those!"

My former colleague Tim Taylor was a news anchor who prided himself on his composure. He recalls his early days in local radio and how eager he was to impress management when he began his big upgrade to Cleveland's WHK. He mellifluously concluded his first newscast with the obligatory area temperature update: "And now, scanning the Cleveland climatological area for Parma, Parma Heights, and Pecker Pipe . . ."

> *Any child can tell you that the sole purpose of a middle name is so he can tell when he's really in trouble.*
>
> —DENNIS FAKES

DICK'S MEMORIES

John, Paul, George, Ringo, and Dick

Our station, Channel 3, was just down the street from Public Hall. In August 1964, we all knew the Beatles were coming. I left the station for the evening and probably headed for The Swamp, where everybody would go to drink lunch, and saw a whole multitude of kids. I thought this was interesting, kept walking, and then got caught up in an avalanche of kids trying to get in the side door of Public Hall. I couldn't move, and finally I thought the only way out was to try to get into that building.

I got to the door, and a girl screamed "Dick Goddard!" The rush was on, and the kids started giving me stuffed animals. "Give these to the Beatles!" They must have had ten stuffed animals they shoved at me. I was at the door, and a guard saw me and said, "Get in here!" I was pushed in the door and pulled inside, and suddenly I'm backstage with the Beatles at Public Hall.

I'm not afraid of hell, I don't believe in it, but back then I had some idea there may have been a hell, and I couldn't fear it because it couldn't have been worse than the noise level there. It was just incredible—and totally illuminated from the nonstop popping of the flashbulbs they used back then.

I was standing just across from the Beatles as they started their performance. The police stopped it after the first song. The shrieking and tumult had to be stopped. They told the audience, "You gotta cut that out or we're going to cut this short." And the show went on.

He also likes to recall the evening that I told weather viewers that we had to be concerned about an onrushing and bitterly cold Canadian air mass. To the delight of viewers, and to my dismay, it came out "a cold mare's ass." Tim put his head down on the desk, and all you could see was the top of his hair.

I put Robin Swoboda on the ropes one evening when they lost a story at the end of the newscast. The director said, "You guys are gonna have to fill because the machine ate the tape. You've got fifteen seconds. What are you gonna do?" We had already talked earlier about Tim's golf game and things like that. I remembered that Larry Richardson of the Lake Erie Science Center had sent me a photograph of a spring peeper, a tiny cricket frog. I had used it on the early show and talked about spring peepers as the gatekeepers of spring—"you don't see them, they're very secretive, but you hear their sleigh bell chorus." I knew we still had the photograph. "Five seconds," the director said. "What are you gonna do?"

Stay tuned, I told Robin and our viewers, and then unfortunately left out a key word: "Coming back I'm going to show you my peeper!" Robin's laser eyes grew to Orphan Annie dimensions, I said, "Oh my goodness," and our director mercifully faded to blue.

Stage performers often come acropper at critical moments. The famous actor Rex Harrison recalled his first role. He played the part of a new father, and at the moment of delivery shouted, "It's a doctor . . . fetch a baby!"

A fine example of a spoonerism at its best came when an aspiring Hollywood actor was introduced to the famous British film star Walter Pidgeon. "Mr. Privilege," gushed the young man, "this is indeed a pigeon."

Spoonerisms have claimed victims from all professions, including presidents of the United States. During the 1976 presidential campaign, President Gerald Ford concluded a speech by declaring "Jimmy Carter speaks loudly and carries a fly spotter . . . a flywasher . . . It's been a long day." And consider these remarks by Vice President George Bush: "For seven and a half years I've worked alongside President Reagan. We've had triumphs, made some mistakes. We've had sex . . . uh . . . setbacks!"

The mixed metaphor is another form of speech dysphasia.

A dog wags its tail with its heart.

In his career as manager of the Cleveland Indians, Charlie Manuel showed promise of becoming the poor man's Yogi Berra. Charlie had a lot of trouble crossing bridges. After one of those uncomfortable postgame interviews, Charlie explained to reporters, "We'll tackle that bridge when we come to it."

After another quizzing, Charlie announced, "We'll jump off that bridge when we come to it."

Charlie summed up the Indians' scoring problems with this explanation: "If we don't score more runs than they do, we're gonna lose."

The Cleveland radio team has done a great job of broadcasting first-place games for an also-ran in recent seasons. I knew that it was going to be a long year when early on I heard Mike Hegan put his meteorological seal of approval in jeopardy by announcing that "it's raining harder now than it was before it started."

I'll conclude with a few of those hilarious linguistic distortions that are known as mondegreens. The word *mondegreen* was coined in 1914 by Sylvia Wright. In a mondegreen, the listener misinterprets words to mean something entirely different from what was intended. A classic example would be hearing "Jose, can you see?" instead of "Oh, say can you see?"

Children, naturally, are most subject to this confusion, and here are some of their precious mondegreens:

"YA WANNA KNOW WHAT THE WEATHER IS? LOOK OUT THE DAMN WINDOW."

There is only one smartest dog in the world, and every boy has it.

God bless America, land that I love,
Stand aside, sir, and guide her,
With delight through the night from a bulb.
Our Father, Art, in heaven, Harold be Thy name.
Thy King done come, Thy will be done,
On Earth as it is in heaven.
Give us this day our jelly bread,
And forgive us our press passes,
As we forgive those who press past against us.
And lead us not into Penn Station,
But deliver us some e-mail.
A-men.

Rocking Robin

I had just left Robin Swoboda's home in Lakewood when I saw a man lying on a tree lawn. I stopped to see if the fellow needed help and half-carried him onto the porch of what I thought was his home. I continued on to work, and it was not long after I arrived that I got a call from a furious woman who asked why I had put a drunk on her porch swing.

When Robin was "available" she had many male fans. She showed me some of the letters that poured in, and I distinctly remember the one from a teenager who said, "At this time I think you are one of the most beautiful women I have ever seen." Nothing is permanent.

Leaving Channel 8 for the Linoleum Room at Wendy's one evening with Robin and Tim, she spied a suitor she wanted to avoid. We drove at a fast clip while Robin was horizontal in the back seat.

Robin was scolded by Channel 5 for jumping out of a cake at Channel 8 during my seventieth birthday celebration. I used the name "Milo Fenoink" when using reports she phoned in with other weather spotters in the audience on my station, by the way.

My favorite is a child's interpretation of the events that gave us our Declaration of Independence:

America was founded by four fathers. Delegates from the original thirteen states formed the Contented Congress. Benjamin Franklin and Thomas Jefferson, a Virgin, were two singers of the Decoration of Independence, which says that all men are cremated equal and are well endowed by their creator.

Robin Swoboda had left the night shift at Channel 8 to co-host The *Morning Exchange* at Channel 5, but she returned to TV8 for my 70th birthday party—jumping out of a cake in which she was smuggled in! I heard later that Channel 5 wasn't happy about it, because she was still under a no-compete clause in her contract.

DICK'S PALS

Miss Julie

Julie Ann Cashel and Dick in a restaurant in Hartville, Ohio—while on a "One Tank Trip" with Neil Zurcher.

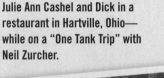

NEIL ZURCHER: Something should be said about Julie—Miss Julie, Julie Ann Cashel—who was the love of Dick's life, and how they met. She called the station one day and said she was a Playboy bunny—or somebody thought she was a Playboy bunny—and she wanted to come in and meet Dick and watch him do the weather. She came in, and she was gorgeous—and very, very nice. It was the late 1960s. Doug Adair was there and I was there. Dick had been divorced, and women were calling, but he hadn't been dating much, and he didn't seem interested. Julie stayed all evening long, watching the news. Afterward, Dick said goodbye to her, and "so nice meeting you," about three times. Finally Doug said, "Richard, why don't you offer to take her home? Why do think she's been waiting around? Why doesn't she have a car?" It was a cue for Dick, because he was oblivious, as usual. So they left, and we all stood in the door of the old TV8 building on Euclid Avenue, watching like parents. They were together after that. She was his soulmate, and she was a very special lady. She remembered everybody's name, she spoke to everybody, made a point of it, and was always there to help a good cause. It was heartbreaking when she died in 1996. She was just a wonderful person.

Longtime reporter and Goddard pal Neil Zurcher (who played a key role in starting the Woollybear Festival) became best known as the "One Tank Trips" reporter, on TV8 and in his series of books.

Known for the Animals

A dog teaches us a lesson in humility.

—NAPOLEON BONAPARTE

JOE BENNY: We were covering a convention in New York, set up in the work areas around Madison Square Garden. At the end of a day, the groups from different stations would get together and BS. Someone asked where we were from, and I said Cleveland. Yeah? What station? WJW.

"Hey," somebody says, "do you have a guy that gives away animals?"

"That's us," I said—"it's Dick Goddard, our meteorologist."

"That's your show? Wow! You guys are known all over the country."

GOSSIP

If you can't say anything nice about someone,
come sit by me.

—Alice Roosevelt Longsworth

You can't be too sensitive in this business. I've gotten some pretty nasty letters over the years. People don't just complain about forecasts—they straighten out your grammar or they criticize your appearance. I know one guy who quit because he just couldn't handle being criticized anymore.

I remember vividly the viciousness of some newspaper columnists toward electronic journalists with our "spray-can hair." Management would tell them to let those TV people have it whenever they could. I understood it: Television was now taking away the newspaper as people's first source of news, and that was really resented. There was great animosity.

It was early October 1996 when I was finally able to return to my job as a weather forecaster at Fox 8 television following the most devastating and depressing period in my life. In only twelve hours, I had lost not only my beloved mother, Doris, but my wonderful soul mate of twenty-four years, Julie Ann.

On my first day back on the air, I had just struggled through the evening

You can't be too sensitive in this business.

Just when the caterpillar thinks the world is ending, it becomes a butterfly.

The exact contrary of what is generally believed is often the truth.

—JEAN DE LA BRUYERE

My sleeves are rolled up. Either it was warm or a storm was coming.

news, when the telephone call came. The woman on the other end said, sarcastically, "I hear you killed your mother and your lady." It was so cruel and stunning that I don't remember if I said anything or just hung up. (Until this writing I had only told my friend and colleague Tim Taylor about the unbelievably inhumane call.)

That first week I was back on the air, a television critic at the *Plain Dealer* complained that I was showing no energy on my weather programs (He was later removed from his job). Being a weather forecaster in Northeast Ohio guarantees that you need to have a thick epidermis, but I still regarded this as the epitome of the mean-spiritedness that has taken over our society.

People have been overwhelmingly nice to me since I first climbed into that lighted metal box some forty-four years ago. Those who are in the public eye, be they entertainers, politicians, or whatever, are juicy and easy targets for the diaper-mouths. It simply goes with the territory.

Gossip has always been a titillating hobby for humans, even though the male of the species would probably deny any involvement. That, of course, is not true.

The word *gossip* comes from the root word *god-sub,* which meant "related" (as in family). From there the word mutated into "talk about those related to us," and eventually into "one who delights in idle talk." Simple, idle talk has since morphed into words that can psychologically maim and destroy.

No one is immune from gossip. Even though it is often totally false, once it has been passed on it is embellished and often develops a life of its own. Gossip is so frequently intriguing and delicious that people believe that it must be true.

I remember a player on the Cleveland Browns who was crucified and ridiculed—behind his back, of course—for his sexual preferences in the 1970s. The stories were fabrications, but it was terrific party talk. I'm sure it made the purveyors of the fable feel so much better about themselves.

In the early 1980s, following painful root canal

surgery, I was prescribed a pain reliever called Zomax (which was subsequently banned by the FDA). Its effect could be seen in my breathing. I began to hyperventilate on television, and it was truly embarrassing. One day I was walking through a shopping mall when a mother and her child approached. As they passed, the little boy said, "My mom says that you're on drugs." Technically that may have been correct, but spreading mean-spirited assumptions like this is just one way that gossip is born.

(For the diaper-mouths among us, I hate to spoil your favorite pastime, but I must tell you I have never taken drugs or nonprescribed medications, I have never been drunk, and no one can say I have a bad temper. I'm just a boring, carbon-based biped.)

It was gossip about his wife that caused a future president of the United States to shoot and kill a man. At the age of twenty-four Andrew Jackson married Rachel Donelson Robards. Because of a legal error, Rachel had technically not been divorced when she and Jackson exchanged vows in 1791. They rectified the problem when they exchanged vows again three years later.

Politics have seldom been honest or ethical, so the rivals of Jackson (known as Old Hickory) began a campaign against him and his wife prior to his election as president in 1828.

An early antagonist of the Jacksons had been Charles Dickinson. According to the code of chivalry followed in 1806, Jackson challenged Dickinson to a duel with pistols at eight paces. Dickinson shot first, with the bullet entering Jackson's breastbone, near his heart. It was not a fatal wound, but it was so close to his vital organs that doctors could not operate. Jackson carried the bullet in his body until his death.

The gentleman's code of the time also forbade returning fire if the opponent's shot was not fatal, but Jackson's fiery temperament ruled. He fired away, but the pistol's hammer failed. Jackson fired again, and the bullet hit Dickinson in the abdomen and went through his body, killing him.

Just before Jackson entered the White House as the seventh president of the United States, his wife—who had a history of heart problems—died of heart

A holiday gathering at Tim Taylor's brought together, clockwise from Tim and me, Gib Shanley, John O'Day, John Telich, Tony Rizzo, Dick Conrad, Scott Reed, and Carl Monday.

"I KNOW IT'S EXACTLY 140 MILLION AND 2 YEARS OLD, MADAME, BECAUSE WHEN I STARTED HERE TWO YEARS AGO I WAS TOLD IT WAS 140 MILLION YEARS OLD."

failure. The strain of being called a harlot, whore, and strumpet—even by ministers in the pulpit—finally took its toll on Rachel.

Whether we admit it or not, all of us gossip in some form. While gossip can be of the good-sport-only-kidding variety, too often it is malicious and harmful. While gossipers generally run little risk of retaliation or reprisal, they can be sued for libel or slander.

It is estimated that we utter an average of thirty-three words every minute that we are in conversation (although I know some who gust to fifty). We all know someone who is the "knife of the party," with a great sense of rumor. We need to remember that thoughts can become words at any moment, and that talk is a verbal boomerang that often comes right back at us.

A harmful truth is better than a useful lie.

—THOMAS MANN

Seal of Approval

The American Meteorological Society established its Seal of Approval program to accredit television forecasters in 1957. Almost 2,000 seals have been granted, and about 700 are considered "active."

Dick Goddard holds number 45.

The next closest on the active list—the only other seal old enough to be in double digits—is number 82, held by Elliot Abrams, who has worked since 1967 for the AccuWeather service. He is heard on radio stations that coincidentally include KYW in Philadelphia, where Dick worked in 1965.

Another coincidence: The late Wally Kinnan, Dick's pal and one-time meteorologist for WKYC-TV, was one of the meteorologists who created the AMS Seal of Approval, when the Ohio native was working at KYW's predecessor in Philadelphia. The first seals were granted alphabetically, and Wally received number 3. Number 1 went to Dr. Francis Davis of Philadelphia's WPVI-TV.

DICK'S PALS

A Little Slip

JOE BENNY: Goddard's doing his segment, talking about snowfall around the country, and he says, "Virginia got nine inches last night." And gives a little smile and an aside, and Taylor started laughing. Then Goddard started laughing, and that was it. He couldn't do the forecast.

A Fast Food Trip

ROBIN SWOBODA: We were all going to dinner one time, the usual fast food, and a guy was going to get me—a friend, not a date—and he was late. We didn't have much time, and even though it wasn't a date I wasn't going to be stood up. I got into the car with Tim and Dick, and as we were pulling out of the station we saw the guy pulling in. Tim was driving, I was in the back, and I hunkered down to the floorboards. And the guy started following us.

We went up South Marginal, then Tim turned up East 55th, and I'm on the floor in the back seat. The guy was still following, so Tim tried to lose him. He turned a few times, wound up in a different part of town, and finally lost him. We went to the Linoleum Room of Wendy's, as Dick called it. We got back to the station, and the phone rang, and it was the guy. I told him we went to dinner, I wasn't going to be stood up, and asked, "Why were you following us?" He said, "I knew you were in the car." I asked how he knew. He said, "Because of the [bleep]-eating grin Dick had on his face when you drove past me."

Dick Delivers in a Pinch

TIM TAYLOR: We had one general manager who would slaughter the English language to the point that it was comical. The four of us—me, Robin, Casey Coleman, and Dick—got called into his front office meeting room with a view of the lake. I can't remember what it was about, but he started talking and was slaughtering sentences left and right. We started laughing. Now, you don't want to laugh in your boss's face. We were shaking, trying to hold it in. Finally he hit one word that was too much. Goddard leaped up and pointed to some bird outside the window—"Oh my goodness, did you see that?"—to divert attention, feigning that this was why we were laughing. The rest of us burst into laughter over nothing, able to let it out. That was a magical moment where Dick saved us.

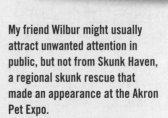

My friend Wilbur might usually attract unwanted attention in public, but not from Skunk Haven, a regional skunk rescue that made an appearance at the Akron Pet Expo.

The Woollybear Festival is for all ages, but some are happier to see me than others.

Pets

It is estimated that seventy thousand puppies and kittens are born each day in the United States. Relatively few find safe, loving homes. Spaying and neutering is the key to helping control the unwanted pet population. Puppies and kittens of both sexes should be spayed or neutered by six months of age. Altering your pet will not only save you money, but allow your friend to live much longer.

"BEFORE I GO I WANT YOU TO BEG, SIT AND ROLL OVER."

Dogs can teach us the true meaning of unconditional love.

How old is your dog?

The old rule of thumb that one dog year equals seven human years is no longer considered valid: A dog is considered to be full grown at twelve months, which equals age eighteen in humans. From that point on you can figure each new year is equal to five human years. An example: if your dog is ten years old, he is sixty-three in human years (nine times five is forty-five, added to eighteen will give you sixty-three).

Ohio's Animal Abuse Law

- A judge can order psychological testing because of the link between animal and human abuse.
- First offense is a misdemeanor punishable by a maximum of six months in jail and a $1,000 fine.
- Second offense is a felony punishable by a maximum of one year in jail and a $2,000 fine.

Fun With Felines

Cats now outnumber dogs in American homes. This has happened because while many homes have just one dog, many have multiple cats. You never truly own a cat, of course. I am owned by four: Sky, Blueberry, Autumn, and Doppler Dot.Com (a high-tech cat). All but Sky are rescues from farms, and two of them have just one eye.

The charm of the cat, to me, is its ultimate independence. Cats are totally honest, and their toughness and ability to survive are legendary. On July 4, 1980, I drove past a little black kitten that had been hit on Detroit Road in Westlake. Not knowing if it was alive, I stopped the car, got out, and held up my hand to stop traffic. The tiny thing was bleeding out of every opening, and at the twenty-four-hour vet's office the opinion was that there was nothing that could be done. Angel lived another nineteen years and died peacefully on Halloween night in 1999.

In ancient Egypt, cats were thought to be gods. Cats have never forgotten this. There are many joys that come with being owned by a cat.

"LET'S WAIT UNTIL HE GETS TO THE SPORTS PAGES."

How to Give a Cat a Pill

Giving a cat a pill is one of the most difficult challenges in life, sort of like shoveling smoke, nailing jelly, or putting socks on a rooster. Here are special techniques you can use to ease a pill down a cat's throat:

1. Pick up cat and cradle in the crook of your arm. Position forefinger and thumb on either side of cat's mouth and gently apply pressure to cheeks while holding pill in free hand. As cat opens mouth, pop pill into mouth. Allow cat to close mouth and swallow.

2. Retrieve pill from floor and cat from behind sofa. Cradle cat in

He wasn't very talkative on his book tour, but Morris the Cat snuggled in close for a photo when he stopped at TV8.

My mom, Doris, almost made it to 91. She and her dog, Trixie, did a promo for TV8 in the '90s, with some nursing assistance.

There are two means of refuge from the miseries of life: music and cats.

—ALBERT SCHWEITZER

arm, holding rear paws tightly. Force jaws open and push pill to back of mouth with forefinger. Hold mouth shut for a count of ten.

3. Retrieve cat from bedroom and throw soggy pill away.

4. Take new pill from foil wrap and call spouse to help. Kneel on floor with cat wedged firmly between knees. Hold front and rear paws. Ignore low growls emitted by cat. Get spouse to hold head firmly with one hand while forcing wooden ruler into mouth. Drop pill down ruler and rub cat's throat vigorously.

5. Retrieve cat from curtains and get another pill from foil wrap (make note to repair torn curtains).

6. Wrap cat in large towel. Get spouse to lie on cat with cat's head just visible from below armpit. Put pill in end of drinking straw, force cat's mouth open with pencil, and blow pill down straw.

7. Check label to make sure pill is not harmful to humans, have a drink to take taste away. Apply bandage to spouse's forearm and remove blood from carpet with plenty of cold water and soap.

8. Consider trading cat for a hamster.

How To Give A Dog A Pill

1. Wrap pill in bacon and give it to dog.

*They are loud, with bad breath and body odor.
I know some dogs that are like that, too.*

Emergency Clinics

Animal Emergency Clinic West, West Cuyahoga. Call for hours of operation.	www.aec.vetsuite.com	216-362-6000
Gateway Animal Clinic, Cleveland (walk-ins). Call for hours of operation.		216-771-4414
Lorain Animal Emergency and Specialty Ctr, open 24 hrs.	www.lcaecc.com	440-240-1400
Metropolitan Veterinary Hospital, Akron, open 24 hrs.	www.metropolitanvet.com	330-666-2976

Emergency Hotlines

Pet FBI: Database of lost and found Ohio pets.	www.PetFBI.org	614-675-1305
Animal Neglect Or Cruelty Hotline.	www.ClevelandAPL.org	216-771-4616
24 Hour National Animal Poison Control Center	www.ASPCA.org/pet-care/poisoncontrol	888-426-4435
Nationwide Pet "Amber Alert"	www.lostmydoggie.com	877-818-0060

501(c) 3 Organizations (nonprofit), County and City Kennels

Adopt Your New Best Friend From One Of The Following Groups!

Alchemy Acres	no kill	www.alchemyacres.org	330-332-4897
Alterpet (low cost spay and neuter)	no kill	www.alterpet.org	330-321-6243
Animals' Disaster Team		www.animalsdisasterteam.org	216-228-1721
Animal Foundation of Cleveland	no kill	www.petfinder.com/shelters/OH149.html	216-861-5255
A New Leash On Life	no kill	www.anewleashonliferescue.org	
Animal Welfare League of Trumbull County	no kill	www.petfinder.com/shelters/OH282.html	330-394-4122
ARC Animal Rescue Center	no kill	www.arc-ohio.org	440-942-1753
Ashtabula County APL	no kill	www.acapl.org	440-224-1222
Ashtabula County Humane Society	no kill	www.achsohio.org	440-969-6100
Ashland County Animal Shelter		www.ashlandcounty.org/dogshelter	419-289-1455
BACK TO THE WILD	no kill	www.backtothewild.com	419-684-9539
Berea Animal Rescue		www.BereaAnimalRescue.com	440-234-2034
Brooklyn Animal Shelter		www.BrooklynShelter.org	216-741-1213
Caroline's Kids Pet Rescue	no kill	www.carolines-kids.org	440-449-3496

Carroll County Humane Society	no kill	www.carrollcountyhumanesociety.org	330-627-3044
C.A.T.S.S.	no kill	www.catssoberlin.org	440-506-5014
City of Cleveland Kennel		http://www.city.cleveland.oh.us	216-664-3069
Cleveland Animal Protective League	no kill	www.clevelandapl.org	216-771-4616
Cuyahoga County Animal Shelter (Valley View)		www.cuyahogadogs.com	216-525-7877
Erie Shores Humane Society	no kill	www.erieshoreshumanesociety.com	440-308-0923
Euclid Pet Pals		www.euclidpetpals.org	216-289-2057
Friends of Pets	no kill	www.waggingtails.org	330-571-7387
Forgotten Animal Shelter (mostly cats)	no kill	www.forgottenanimalshelter.org	330-769-1323
Friendship APL (Lorain County)	no kill	www.friendshipAPL.org	440-322-4321
Geauga Humane Society–Rescue Village	no kill	www.geaugahumane.org	440-338-4819
Golden Treasures (Golden Retrievers)	no kill	www.goldentreasuresrescue.org	FAX: 440-238-2457
Geauga County Dog Shelter (Chardon)	no kill	www.petfinder.com/shelters/OH272.html	440-286-8135
Give Pets a Chance (therapeutic riding)	no kill	www.givepetsachance.org	330-264-3959
Greyhound Adoption	no kill	www.greyhoundadoptionofoh.org	440-543-6256
GRIN (Golden Retrievers)	no kill	www.grinrescue.org	216-556-4746
Happy Tails Cat Sanctuary	no kill	www.petfinder.com/shelters/OH606.html	440-759-0076
Happy Trails Farm Animals Sanctuary	no kill	www.happytrailsfarm.org	330-296-5914
Honuchan Pet Sanctuary	no kill	www.petfinder.com/shelters/OH228.html	
Holmes County Humane Society	no kill	www.holmeshumane.org	330-674-7387
Humane Society of Erie County	no kill	www.humanesocietyoferiecounty.org	419-626-6220
Humane Society of Greater Akron	no kill	www.summithumane.org	330-487-0333
Humane Society of Ottawa County	no kill	www.petfinder.org/shelters/OH187.html	419-734-5191
Huron County Humane Society	no kill	www.hc-humanesociety.org	419-663-7158
Kitten Krazy	no kill	www.kittenkrazy.org	330-421-4203
Lake County Humane Society	no kill	www.lakehumane.org	440-951-6122
Lake Erie Lab Retriever Rescue	no kill	www.lakeerielabrescue.org	419-885-2471
Lake Erie Nature & Science Center (Rehab)	no kill	www.lensc.org	440-871-2900
Lakewood Animal Shelter		www.cclas.info	216-529-5020
Lorain County Dog Kennel	no kill	www.loraincounty.us/dogs	440-326-5995
Lorain County SPCA	no kill	www.spcaloraincty.com	440-233-6771
Love-A-Stray	no kill		216-314-0321
Medina County Animal Shelter (92.8 percent adoption rate)		www.co.medina.oh.us/animal/animal.htm	330-725-9121
Medina County SPCA	no kill	www.medinacountyspca.com	330-723-7722

NewfNeighborhood	no kill	www.lovenewfs.com/nn/	
North Coast Animals	no kill		216-228-1721
North Coast Humane Society	no kill		216-661-2292
Northeast Ohio Collie Rescue	no kill	www.neocr.org	216-213-6197
Northeast Ohio SPCA	no kill	www.northeastohiospca.org	216-351-7387
Oasis Animal Shelter (dogs only)	no kill	www.oasisanimalshelter.net	440-775-4101
One of a Kind Pet Rescue (low cost spay and neuter)	no kill	www.oneofakindpets.com	330-865-6200
Parma Animal Shelter	no kill	www.parmashelter.org	440-885-8014
Parrot Hope Rescue	no kill	www.parrothope.org	330-221-0049
Paws and Prayers	no kill	www.pawsandprayers.org	330-475-8300
Petshelter	no kill	www.northeastohiospca.org	216-351-7387
Place A Pet Foundation	no kill	www.placeapetfoundation.com	216-521-7387
Portage County APL	no kill	www.portageapl.org	330-296-4022
Project Noah/Gateway Clinic		www.projectnoahsavethepets.org	216-771-4414
Public Animal Welfare	no kill	www.pawsohio.org	440-442-7297
Richland County Humane Society		www.adoptourstrays.com	419-774-4795
Rose's Rescue	no kill	www.rosesrescue.net	330-325-0582
Sanctuary for Senior Dogs	no kill	www.sanctuaryforseniordogs.org	216-485-9233
Save Ohio Strays	no kill	www.saveohiostrays.org	440-567-3585
Skunk Haven	no kill	www.skunkhaven.net	440-327-4349
SPCA of Grafton (Lorain County)	no kill	SPCA@windstream.net	440-233-6771
Spelko-Pal Rescue	no kill	www.petfinder.com/shelters/OH241.html	216-351-6982
Stay-A-While Cat Shelter	no kill	www.stayawhilecatshelter.org	440-582-4990
St. Francis Animal Sanctuary	no kill	www.SaintFrancisAnimalSanctuary.org	440-897-2662
Stark County Humane Society	no kill	www.starkhumane.org	330-453-5529
STUMP HILL FARM (exotic animal rescue)	no kill	Massillon	330-833-8402
Tuscarawas Dog Warden		www.co.tuscarawas.oh.us/Commissioners/DogPound.htm	330-339-2616
Valley Save-A-Pet	no kill		440-232-9124
Wayne County Humane Society		www.wchs.org	330-262-0152
Western Reserve Humane Society		www.petfinder.com/shelters/OH450.html	216-481-7332
Wolfspirit's Toy Breed Puppy Mill Rescue	no kill	www.wolfspiritsrescue.com	330-453-2746

When all else fails, read the instructions.
—AGNES ALLEN

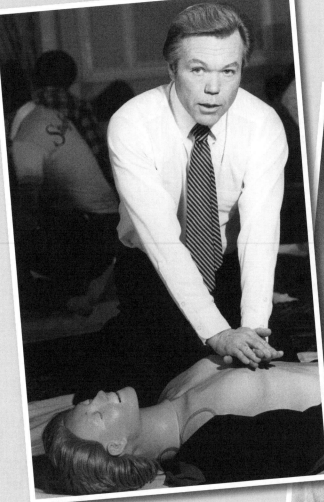

(Dick Goddard photos from Cleveland Press
Collection, Cleveland State University Archives)

Hooters Calendar 2011

JANUARY	FEBRUARY	MARCH	APRIL
S M T W T F S	S M T W T F S	S M T W T F S	S M T W T F S
1	1 2 3 4 5	1 2 3 4 5	1 2
2 3 4 5 6 7 8	6 7 8 9 10 11 12	6 7 8 9 10 11 12	3 4 5 6 7 8 9
9 10 11 12 13 14 15	13 14 15 16 17 18 19	13 14 15 16 17 18 19	10 11 12 13 14 15 16
16 17 18 19 20 21 22	20 21 22 23 24 25 26	20 21 22 23 24 25 26	17 18 19 20 21 22 23
	27 28	27 28 29 30 31	24 25 26 27 28 29 30

DICK GODDARD WORD SEARCH

```
T G Q N C T A N I M A L S H E L T E R X U B G T E B C Q W T
C I L S U G K S L K G E Z V G N J F S A N M O R B U O K Y J
L F M N E O V J H X U V C D F V U W R P Q R T Z P C M F C V
L D A T J I X U K M E F I W E Q E A N J N L F J T K M G P O
K U S J A A P E L I S P X G O N D S T A E Z W C W E X Q M K
V U T A G Y M P M I S P E R O A R J D B E C Y Y J Y T J T D
K E R L L M L Z U C B T A I R S W O W Z O O Y X W E F K H A
F N O N Y B W O O P A O H D F G M O J F L L D O T E G Z J S
Y M N S T I E R R I O B R F T N G O K R D W L V W J Z L N
E R O Z N S O R I Y W K A B H S R K P X K A Y P I L H A T Z
F A M D C O I A T Q A C R G L K B O U A Z I H F Q H T M S K
D X Y H I A N G H A C P I L W E G Y Q R G R Q S K E P T I C
O K F W D L R U O U C E S M A E H D E O R M Y P R F U H M O
P U E Z S R M T M L H L A S G K A E G R K A N E U T E R M I
P V S E G M A U O R O J I H W Q E T A G A S P V S U P A H S
L D U M C N L D P O C R O P Y I K E H D O S S R Q F B C H C
E N W U S A C R D L N U O S P H N K F E L T X Q M M L O N L
R G E H T B E F E O L S P E O E F T Z F R B I N Z S W E B I
R J N I G S S V M A G O U M T O R H E O E M N R O E E X D M
M O O I S Q E Y R A O V G B R E A V P R K C A H R R Z W P A
W N N U T L W D I N O N R V F O M S E Q U I T N G L D W L T
Z E R B A S I E E S P L P F V K T P T A Q C T R A L Y I A E
I E A N O N A R N E N F W C S E O S X A B Y L T S N S L E R
E E D T T T I C P E J A O Z A Z R Z R R T R Q O E Z D M P Z
L D N Q H S Z P D I W O I R M P G M G E A I O Z U N K A S D
O L X E M E V W F A U E W D E W K W I A D A S W V D S S L D
J B D Y K R R L Q Y O M T T N C P I E L E N T T N X Y M Q R
C L N C U Y A H O G A R S A I I A F K I I F U Q I S G I F Q
C R U L S X K D O V T M B H K J V S M C R O T H D C T T W O
H E W O O L L Y B E A R U S J L Y O T C A E N F T W S H M Y
```

Words can appear horizontal, vertical, diagonal, and backwards. Good luck!

ACCUMULATION	CLEVELAND	ERIE	METEOROLOGIST	SKEPTIC	VEGETARIAN
ALBERTACLIPPER	CLIMATE	FORECAST	NEUTER	SNOWBELT	VERMILION
ANIMALSHELTER	CLOUDY	GHOULARDI	NEWS	SPAY	WEATHER
ASTRONOMY	COLDAIRMASS	GODDARD	OHIO	SPOONERISM	WEATHERMAN
BOBBLEHEAD	CUYAHOGA	GREEN	PETS	SPORTS	WILMASMITH
BROADCASTING	DOPPLER	GUESS	PRESSURE	STATISTICS	WINDY
BROWNS	EIGHT	INDIANS	PUPPIES	THUNDERSTORM	WINTER
BUCKEYE	EMMY	KITTENS	RADAR	TIMTAYLOR	WJWTV
CARTOONS	ENEWETAK	LAKEEFFECT	SHOWER	TORNADO	WOOLLYBEAR

WHAT DO YOU CALL A GROUP OF WEATHERMEN?

If a group of lions is a pride and a group of geese is called a gaggle, what do you call a group of weathermen? A *guess!* And that's what they had at a Landerhaven Corporate Club luncheon early in 2007 when Mark Nolan of WKYC, Don Webster of WEWS, and Mark Johnson of WEWS joined me and Jon Loufman of WOIO/WUAB (he's not in the photo) to talk about forecasting. They were obviously proud to display their "Trust in Goddard" T-shirts, and you'll even notice Webster giving the Hawaiian good-luck sign. Johnson tugged at my hair at one point and said, "Nolan, you owe me twenty bucks—it's real." Webster, who was already retired and served as moderator, asked me if I called Noah or if Noah called me when the big flood came. "Noah was two years ahead of me in high school," I said, "so he called me."

TOP TEN REASONS FOR BEING A TELEVISION METEOROLOGIST . . .

10. You can never get lost—people are always telling us where we can go.

9. It's a good thing to belong to a nonprophet organization.

8. It's one of the few jobs where you can climb the ladder of success wrong-by-wrong.

7. To anyone who annoys you with a trite "Looks like a nice day," you can counter with a snappy "Not if that trough at 500 millibars continues to amplify."

6. In only three minutes you can irritate nearly everybody in twenty-five counties.

5. Weather people traditionally get to referee newsroom food fights.

4. You can blame bad forecasts on caterpillar larvae and large marmots.

3. Hanging out with Slider, Moondog, and Robin Swoboda.

2. On your eightieth birthday you'll only be 27 Celsius.

1. Management has no idea what you do.

WEATHER FORECASTER'S

ODE

Now among the fading embers,
These in the main are my regrets:
When I'm right no one remembers,
When I'm wrong no one forgets.

(Thank you, Grantland Rice.)

"PEOPLE USED TO HAVE TO LOOK OUT THE WINDOW TO TELL WHAT THE WEATHER WAS."